# A DIFFERENT STAGE

# A DIFFERENT
# GARY BARLOW STAGE

MICHAEL  JOSEPH

PENGUIN MICHAEL JOSEPH

UK | USA | Canada | Ireland | Australia | India | New Zealand | South Africa

Penguin Michael Joseph is part of the Penguin Random House group of companies
whose addresses can be found at global.penguinrandomhouse.com

First published by Penguin Michael Joseph, 2022
001

Set in Alternate Gothic & Plantin
Studio Fury
Printed in Italy by Printer Trento Ltd S.r.L.
Colour reproduction by Altaimage Ltd.

The authorized representative in the EEA is Penguin Random House Ireland, Morrison
Chambers, 32 Nassau Street, Dublin D02 YH68

A CIP catalogue record for this book is available from the British Library

ISBN: 978–1–405–95273–6

www.greenpenguin.co.uk

Penguin Random House is committed to a
sustainable future for our business, our readers
and our planet. This book is made from Forest
Stewardship Council® certified paper.

Never forget where you've come here from
Never pretend that it's all real
Someday soon this will all be
someone else's dream
This will be someone else's dream.

'Never Forget', Take That

6

# CONTENTS

# PREFACE

*by Gary Barlow*

When I started working on *A Different Stage* I was nearly 50. Turning 50 is a reflective time in anyone's life. At 50 you're kind of forced by the shape of the number to take stock and wonder what your life's all been about, and where it's going.

With a milestone birthday on the horizon I felt I needed to do something to mark it, something new. Should I go to Tibet and sit with monks in silence? I didn't fancy skydiving. The pandemic meant I'd have to do both by Zoom anyway. How to mark this stage in my life?

I'm at an interesting point. I've been around a long time, as an artist. Take That had their first *Smash Hits* cover in 1991. Some of you might feel like this bloody fella's been sat somewhere in your house for a lifetime. (Sorry about that.)

Do I keep on making albums? I've got such an amazing audience I could easily do that, but it's not challenging because I will always make music anyway, it's in my DNA. Making music is one of my vital signs. If I stop making music then I'm ill.

I needed a challenge.

For the audience, *A Different Stage* is a good night out, I hope. For me, it's frightening, it is way beyond what is comfortable for me. It's significantly easier for me to get up and sing and dance in front of 80,000 people at Wembley than to perform an intimate one-man show like this.

*A Different Stage* required a new skill.

So why am I doing this?

I love telling a story, all my friends know that. That side of me has always been hidden from an audience, though, because for me that wasn't what performing was about. Words were for lyrics, and spoken words were something I used as a quick bridge to get to another song. The songs were everything.

Then, a few years ago in 2018, I narrated the audio version of my autobiography. I remember doing it a bit reluctantly, but I knew I couldn't leave it to a professional. No one could be more professional at being me than me.

As you get older not many things surprise you, but I was taken aback by how much I loved reading my story out loud. There was an intimacy about someone listening to me tell my story myself that went beyond what you get from reading on the page. I realised storytelling is as primal a thing as music.

I wanted to explore how I could use this storytelling on the stage.

At the time, everyone was talking about Bruce Springsteen on Broadway. It was a bit of a thing, musicians in theatres reading from a memoir, talking and singing, perhaps showing a few slides. After ten minutes watching Bruce I thought, 'It's good, but my show's not going to be like this.'

Songs and a chat felt too serious for someone like me.

I went on a bit of a dive into one-man shows.

In the Victorian theatres, they were apparently put on in the interval by out-of-work actors as a kind of living CV. But in my mind, it's not just a theatre thing, it's not just about Willy Russell's amazing *Shirley Valentine*, it includes Peter Kay's stand-up and Frank Sinatra holding the audience in his hand as he banters between songs. And Noël Coward, the musician, actor and playwright, whose solo shows featured him telling funny stories, playing piano, and all in an exceedingly droll way.

I looked at all of these historical shows, I even went to Pompeii where there was a theatre in Roman times dedicated to one-man shows, and tried to absorb some of that ancient magic. I became fascinated by the whole history and concept of one person on stage.

Clearly I'm not Noël Coward, whose work was literary as much as musical, but the more I dug, the more I felt drawn to try.

There was one show that I loved. Carrie Fisher – the actress who played Princess Leia in *Star Wars* – was the daughter of two Hollywood stars, the actress Debbie Reynolds and the singer Eddie Fisher. I think I've had a life, but blimey, she really did. Carrie's one-woman show, *Wishful Drinking*, was brilliant, and her tone much more my bag. She didn't mind the laugh being on her, she never self-congratulated, she was not afraid of emotion or failure.

A one-man show is the absolute antithesis of what I do on stage during a concert. Being behind a piano is what I do naturally. Standing up and talking is not my natural habitat. It scared the life out of me as much as it thrilled me.

I thought about this for around a year, then I decided to act. I'd need help. I talked to Tim Firth, the composer and writer I've worked with on two musicals: *Calendar Girls* and *The Band*. I first met Tim when I was still at school. He's never forgotten the jumper I was wearing. I've never forgotten his strange coat.

Tim knows me really well. The first thing he said was, 'Why are you doing this? You can't just rattle on about all your awards and the fun you've had on tour, that'll be rubbish. You'll have to go somewhere you've never been before. Where's that?'

We started working on this during the first lockdown in 2020, with me writing great chunks of detail about my life and then the two of us setting about deciding which parts belonged in a two-hour show. We were absolutely merciless and reduced it down to crucial people, places, moments and music. It was like a puzzle, putting the pieces of my life together.

Once we had that, it was time to start learning how to present it. The learning was a big thing, all-consuming. The scary part wasn't the discipline of learning the shape of the show and the words – that was hard work and I am not afraid of graft. What terrified me was the performance. I was comfortable going through everything in my head but the fear set in when I started saying the words out loud.

Doing new things that frighten me is exciting. I admit it, I don't think I had ever seen a play in my life until Tim asked me to come and see *Calendar Girls* about ten years ago.

I said, 'Will there be music?'

He said, 'It's a play, Gary.'

I said, 'Surely it'd be better with a bit of music.'

He was right, it was a good play. It deserved its standing ovation from the audience. I was excited to watch an audience react. Be moved. Laugh.

If I hadn't had the experience of writing for musicals, I could never have written *A Different Stage*. There's a whole new routine to 'treading the boards', as they say in the theatre. It was a whole new way of taking an audience on a journey.

Before I go on stage, even Wembley Stadium, there's no drama. We don't treat it like an art, we don't talk about 'my craft'. I might do a few star jumps, but I treat my voice like an instrument. I warm it up, I give it lots of sleep, I limit how much I talk, but then, when it comes to being on stage, I go out and have fun. I've been doing this for over forty years now, I'm an old pro.

Sitting backstage on Broadway and in the West End, the preparation is silent, meditative. Preparing for this show, I need to go very still and quiet. This is new. It's exercised me. It's taken me far outside my comfort zone.

I have lived with the show's words for over two years now, as I am writing this.

At first it was just reading, then I'd be talking the show through in the car, in bed before I went to sleep, whenever I was alone, while I was walking the dogs. The great composer Hans Zimmer says you should always write with a metronome – the musician in me had to figure out the beat in the sentences.

With spoken words there are still the highs and lows of a voice, like singing. As I grew more comfortable I started to see the words as beats. Eventually I could hear an imaginary underscore, a faint background music that reflected the mood or the meaning in the words I was speaking. Thinking about words like music helped. Words, just like music, translate feelings.

This whole process has been one scary thing after another, but remembering the words was very scary. I can't remember anything. 'Hi Gary, I'm Bob.' 'Hi, er, what did you say your name was again?' I can't even remember my own lyrics. At first it took me two weeks to learn ten minutes, by the end I could learn half an hour of words in two days.

The human brain is still trainable, even at 50. Neuroplasticity, they call it.

There are other essential elements to a show. Set, lights, sound, costume. Over the years I've worked with incredible professionals who are right at the top of their craft. Those people are part of this production too. People like Tim, and like Es Devlin who has been our set designer on the huge multimillion-pound Take That tours that we've done, and who made my day when she agreed to do this little show.

I work with the best, what a joy that is, what a privilege. But there's a home-made aspect too. We've got no costume designer. I've done all the clothes. I bought all the old British Knight jackets and Fila trainers from eBay. Dawn sewed the pockets into the big jumper for the balloons we use to create a bigger me in the wilderness years.

I've literally worked with friends and family.

So no, I didn't fancy jumping out of a plane, I did something much harder. This process has been like learning Chinese, a helluva challenge. I couldn't count the hours I have spent on this. Even asleep, it's there. I've had a lot of very intense dreams.

*A Different Stage* opened in Runcorn at the Brindley Theatre a couple of weeks after my 51st birthday and a short walk from the first working men's club to give me a residency. I'd go there after school aged 14. I wanted it to be in rep up north, where I'm from, in small theatres that are up close where I can talk to the audience. The run ended at Frodsham Community Centre, in the town where I was born and bred, where my mum and brother, and Tim Firth, my co-writer, still live.

It's normal to run away from where you're from, but for me it was time to go back. *A Different Stage* is about people, and Frodsham's where my life started. It felt right to go back there; plus the son and brother in me wanted to surprise Mum and Our Ian. I hope I've surprised you too.

# INTRODUCTION

*by Tim Firth, Director and Co-writer*

Gary and I are friends. I can vividly remember the schoolboy that turned up to BBC Pebble Mill the first time I met him, not least because he was wearing the most peculiar jumper.

Fast forward thirty-five years and we've written two musicals together and now *A Different Stage*.

Anybody on the planet could have a story written about their life because every human life is fascinating, whether the person in question realises it or not. The person you are today is a composite of everything you've seen, loved, loathed, everything that's hurt, impressed or enthralled you. It all adds up to who you are now. A life story is a series of pivotal individual stories, a chain of events.

*A Different Stage* is about those stories in Gary's life. We tend to think of our famous figures as a sequence of singles, tours, and the occasional tabloid scandal. But that's not a human life.

Gary's had a life like nobody else's. As a kid he had his dream, and he got to live it out in spades, and then he lost that dream and began to live a nightmare. But not only did he get his dream back, he got it back bigger than it was the first time. That's incredibly rare.

Those of us lucky enough to get something a second time around can approach life with the wisdom gained from failure. Gary's story, it's almost Shakespearean. He went deep into some very dark woods, experienced his long dark night of the soul and came out a better person.

I don't believe Gary was a bad person the first time, but he freely admits his arrogance, the hubris, the pride that came before the fall. His gratitude for what he has now is so enhanced for it. Even though he's a different person, it's the same guy. Gary mark one built Gary mark two.

I know Gary doesn't see himself as a role model, I'd take the piss out of him if he did. But there's no doubting there are life lessons in his story. It would have been very easy for him to give up when his career tanked – he'd already realised his dream, he had enough money in the bank. For a while he fell into the abyss. He deeply felt his failure, he was depressed, obese, he felt a horrible confusion and I'd go as far as to say I think he felt shame. But he didn't give up, he was held up by the love for his family and his love for music.

That's a story all right.

Fair play to him. He learned the lessons from the dark time. After the ten-year hiatus, the interregnum, he went on to write more music shaped by that experience. Gary's life story is a self-rescue story, it is a redemption story. But it's got a theatrical narrative. Usefully, it also comes with a pretty awesome ready-made soundtrack.

Gary has a performer's ego, of course he does, but there is a genuine humility and wisdom there. His great strength is that he's grown up and he's learned lessons. Very often, once people have made their mistakes, they have to live with those mistakes for the rest of their lives. Gary had the chance, and the humility, to go back and rebuild.

When he started talking about wanting to do this, I never hesitated. It was clear from the start this wasn't going to be an ego bath. That is not what *A Different Stage* is.

Gary is not an actor. He's him being him. But all the time it's a poised monologue with music. The closest thing I can compare it to is Willy Russell's play *Shirley Valentine*.

When we started working I said, 'Start writing, write down what the opening of the show would be.'

That first section was huge. It was a zip file that I opened and it filled the room. From his source material, I'd write a section, return it to him and then he'd read it, record it, and send it back to me. This was in the early part of lockdown and while everyone else was making sourdough we had this daily process.

Once we had his life roughly down, we set about honing it into shape. I was brutal. We both were. We chopped out loads. Anything I felt I already knew about was out.

What should we include? Take That, as a band, is only a tiny part of what else is going on in his life off stage. We spend almost as much time on the kid Barlow eating his pick 'n' mix as we do on the band.

This is about those bits of Gary that are usually hidden. We don't need to tell people what happened with the band because they were there.

People are surprised at the way *A Different Stage* rips along, whether he's dealing with the trauma of death or discussing the wheels on his first BMX. The show bounces along with the same fizzing and aerated pace. This is storytelling. The teller can't be emotive.

He's not asking for sympathy. He's not asking for your forgiveness.

It's a story. It's up to you, the audience, what you take from it.

*A Different Stage* works because I've known Gary so long. I was able to easily tap into his voice rhythms and turns of phrase. We couldn't have done this if we weren't great friends.

In some ways, we are very different. In the first years of him being a pop star, I was at Cambridge University. When he was packing out arenas in his cycling shorts, I was writing plays for Alan Ayckbourn up in Scarborough.

In other ways, we are the same. We both come from the same corner of England in Cheshire, there's our shared forensic fascination with what makes a good show. Plus, he's the only person I know with quite the same appetite for work.

Northern blokes don't love their mates in any way that you'd notice. That's not how it works in the north. We show our feelings by just constantly taking the piss. And Gary and I *constantly* take the piss out of each other. If we ever start being polite to each other I'll be worried.

# ACT I

# ACT I

## GARY BARLOW: BORN AT NUMBER ONE

*And now, the man you've been waiting for . . .*

There were four Gary Barlows born in 1971 and I am relieved to report that I was the first. I was the number one Gary Barlow of 1971.

Not that it makes being called Gary any better. I hate my name but it's a bit late to be changing it now.

Marjorie Barlow had to quickly find a name and she wasn't going to fuss over the decision. 'It was a rushed affair because I was convinced I was having a girl and was dead set on Gillian. I really wanted a girl. I didn't really like any boys' names. Guy was on the cards, but I was talked out of that by my mother. She didn't like Guy, thought it was too grown up a name for a little baby, and I think she was right. It suits you, Gary.'

Thanks, Mum, a great improvement.

There were actually five of us with the same name born that year if you include Garry Barlow. Flash beggar. I wonder if I'd have felt better about my name if I'd a jazzy extra R?

It's got worse over time as the name's grown more and more dated. Its moment was brief. 1944, 100th most popular boy's name. 1954: 39th. In 1964 it was 16th. By 1974 it dropped back down the 'hit parade' to 35. In 2020 it was the 2,076th most popular male name in the country.

Some names come back into fashion but there's no way on earth Gary will ever be back. Let's hope not, anyway. Kids should be protected from it.

Mum remembers the song 'Grandad' being on the radio a lot around the time the number one Gary was born, 'But I didn't really take too much notice of it. It was a bit of a busy time. Decent music seemed thin on the ground in 1971.'

Yes, in addition to being called Gary, number one in the charts on the day I was born was Clive Dunn's 'Grandad' song (B-side: 'I Play the Spoons'). Dunn played the doddery old Lance Corporal Jones in *Dad's Army*, and looks like an 80-year-old in the show, so he was hardly a rival for Marc Bolan. In fact he was younger than I am now when he recorded 'Grandad'.

Anyone who knows this song will be like me in wondering if the song was a joke, because it was written by Herbie Flowers, the bass player on Lou Reed's 'Walk on the Wild Side', a very cool song produced by David Bowie and Mick Ronson.

Still, that was number one the week the first Gary Barlow of 1971 was born in a Runcorn hospital. And it goes to show that music is a very broad church, a wide, wide world with plenty of room for someone called Gary.

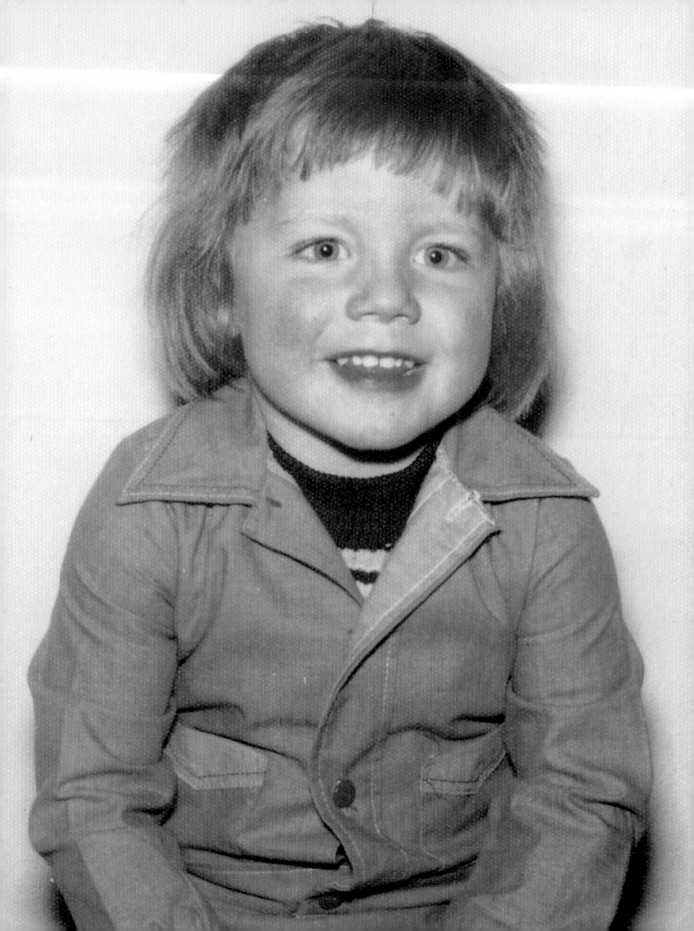

## 'RHINESTONE COWBOY'

*From that moment on, I spent all my pocket money on records.*

My first favourite record was 'Rhinestone Cowboy' by Glen Campbell. It was different to what was floating round my little world at the time; there wasn't a lot of American country music being played on Radio Merseyside in 1975.

Most country music is very pleasing to the ear with amazing musicians brushing and stroking their instruments and casual storytelling vocals. Country tends not to be over-sung or over-played – it's just very 'fireside' and natural.

Glen Campbell's 'Rhinestone Cowboy', like any great tune, just captured me. It captured a lot of other people too, and was the first song in a generation to top both the country charts and the Hot 100 in the US. That's what you call a crossover smash.

I often wonder how my mind would have heard it before I'd trained my ears to pick music apart. I guess a 4-year-old me heard Glen Campbell's 'Rhinestone Cowboy' as one big sound. Who knows, maybe it was as simple as that lyrical link to cowboys?

One thing's for sure, at that young age I wouldn't have been admiring Glen's exceptional guitar playing or deconstructing the arrangement. As a songwriter and record-maker now, I still love the song. What's not to like? But I appreciate it at a whole other level. It's beautifully engineered and mixed, has amazing vocals and is a true classic.

The pathos in those real-life lyrics is touching, as this down-at-heel musician with his subway fare stuffed in his shoe wanders the streets of Broadway, hoping for a brighter future when he'll be 'Like a rhinestone cowboy at a star-spangled rodeo'.

# PICK 'N' MIX

*Stage directions: sit on front of stage with a sweetie bag.*

Saturday morning, 10am, every week, my dad pulled 10p from the back pocket of his jeans and gave it me. He wore his jeans with a belt, the same brown belt he wore for forty years. I watched every motion like a hawk, held my little hand out and he dropped the 10p from his shovel-sized hand into mine.

That 10p was the door to the weekend. I'd throw on my snorkel parka (those snorkel parkas were built for US airmen during the Korean War to protect them from the harshest of weather conditions, but by the seventies and eighties they were being worn by every single schoolboy in Britain) and leg it down to the newsagents so fast the coin would still be warm from my dad's pocket when I handed it over. Here, under a glass counter, was a technicolour world of sugar. The pick 'n' mix.

This was back in a time when you could get a lot of sweets for 10p.

What you chose to put in that pink and white stripy bag was uniquely you, like a glucose fingerprint. What to choose? I picked and mixed up the cola bottles, liquorice pipes, Sherbet Dip Dab, fried eggs, those spongy false teeth, Space Dust and Refreshers, and a little roll of Parma Violets.

Looming over the glass counter with mouths pinched like a cat's bum were the miserable couple who owned the shop. Clearly, they hated kids. It was one of those shops that sold everything: tennis sets, AA maps, toys, racks and racks of magazines that as I got more and more into music were the gateway to information I craved.

These two stood there and for a moment I wanted to run out of the shop in fear but then the enticing aromas hit my nose and they drew me in like a magnet. Boiled sugar, cheap chocolate and a mingling of all the synthetic flavourings, rhubarb and custard, parma violet, vanilla, strawberry, banana, pear drops, toffee, fudge . . .

Once I had that bag, I headed off to the park with an inner glow, knowing what was rustling around inside the pocket of my parka.

The concept of pick 'n' mix comes from America, obviously, where all the good things come from when you're a kid. It was first introduced to the US in the late-nineteenth century in a new chain of value stores called Woolworths. It first opened in Britain in Liverpool, 1909. 'Woollies', as it was always known to Brits, used to import 'candy' from New York until Irish and British factories were able to make them some proper sweets.

The rest is diabetic history in waiting.

# A SMALL TOWN IN THE NORTH OF ENGLAND

*The beautiful town of Frodsham in Cheshire.*

Frodsham (population 9,000) is on the English border with Wales and almost exactly halfway between the great British cities of Manchester and Liverpool.

Up on Frodsham Hill, the view is pretty epic. There are these big skies overlooking the whole town of Frodsham, the high street, the market on a Thursday, Runcorn, the Fiddler's Ferry power station, the M56, the Mersey estuary as it empties into the Irish Sea. On a clear day you'd see Liverpool: the planes flying in and out of Speke Airport, and if you know what you're looking for you can actually see both cathedrals, Catholic and Protestant.

But behind it to the east, it's farming as far as the eye can see. Always has been. Cheshire potatoes mostly. It's why my dad was so into farming, it's what our little town is all about. Even when I got really famous Mum and Dad sold potatoes at their gate, and eggs. 'Take That eggs,' Nigel Martin-Smith used to call them.

Frodsham was a hot tourist destination hundreds of years ago. A century before Blackpool was even dreamed of, people came to 'take the air' and have an afternoon tea and a ride on the helter skelter.

It's probably sleepier now in my home town than it was 200 years ago. There are thirty buildings on Main Street with one of those blue plaques. And it has an even longer history. Alongside the sweethearts' initials etched into the rust-red rock on Frodsham Hill there is even older graffiti going back to the Bronze Age when people started moving to the area.

A Roman road ran through Frodsham, towards the ports on the Mersey, Chester and Manchester, but my home town really came to life in medieval times about a thousand years ago.

The fact that **I** constantly wanted to leave doesn't mean it's not a lovely place.

Frodsham was the <u>perfect</u> beginning.

We're in the Domesday Book and Frodsham is laid out like a typical medieval town. We're famous for our wide main street, wide enough to turn an ox cart round when you're coming in to the market, which is still going on a Thursday. An ox doesn't have reverse like a horse does, and an ox cart was like the Land Rover of its time: good over rough terrain.

The fact that I constantly wanted to leave doesn't mean it's not a lovely place. Frodsham was the perfect beginning. Not all kids gaze longingly at the horizon, at motorways and ports, or talk about capital cities, and dream of blue skies and America. I did. I think I was always contemplating adventures in a bigger world. Before those adventures happen, though, it helps to grow up safe and secure.

I was surrounded by hard-working adults trying to bring their kids up. If Mum wasn't home, the neighbour took us in. If the little kids needed looking after, the big kids stepped in. I had really great mates too.

The town had a nice school. And I was protected by an older brother, Ian, who also happened to be, briefly, the town bad boy. If I think about what I took from that town first and foremost though, it was that you work hard – that life wasn't about luck – life was about putting in the effort and the hours. These were my building blocks.

Walking to school in the morning, all I'd see around me were people with long faces going off to work. That northern grimace doesn't mean times are bad. It's the standard northern factory setting. The seventies and eighties were a time when laughter was a weekly privilege reserved for the last few hours of the pub on a Friday night. Smiling was for game-show hosts.

It's a toss up between me and Daniel Craig when it comes to Frodsham's most famous son. Daniel Craig's dad ran one of the town's pubs. I wonder if he had a long face. Town lawyer, mechanic, teacher, chemical plant worker, farmer, shopkeeper. They were all the same. You didn't show your feelings.

Frodsham's an old market town, and in the centre some of the buildings are old old. Like, fourteenth-century old. Its main street looks like a quaint kid's picture book idea of what a high street looks like. There are no big chain stores, the shop's owner may well serve you. It's old-fashioned like that.

Our first house was in a small street on a relatively new estate that was a mix of council and cheap houses, all small, red brick and right on the edge of town.

Ashton Drive was a good street where people spent their whole lives. You didn't move house. Why would you?

When I was aged 4, my brother and I were sat down and asked our opinion for the first time ever.

'Should I go back to work?' Mum asked us.

'No,' we said, 'stay here and look after us.'

My parents decided not to pay any attention to our opinion, and she went back to work as a laboratory technician anyway. By the time I was 12, eight years of hard work on, we moved to London Road. *How dare they?* people thought. *That means they've done well, that they've got aspirations.* As if that was a bad thing.

London Road was all semis and detached houses and a massive step up for my parents, who had grafted to get there. I can't say I noticed the difference at that age. To me, the only advantage was I could leave home at 8.30, not 8.15, because we were closer to school.

My parents' friends from our old street still popped in for tea. Mum and Dad didn't have social aspirations, they didn't change their lives. They weren't trying to escape who they were, they were just trying to take care of their family.

I did thirty-three years in and around Frodsham. I didn't leave for London until the mid-noughties. Even when Take That were at their nineties peak, I stayed near the town I was born in. Mum and Our Ian still live there.

When I go home everyone's keen to come and chat and congratulate me. Which is lovely, really lovely, but popping out for milk can take hours.

Like my mum, my brother's happy there. London or Manchester are good for 'a night out' but then he wants to come home to the countryside.

Fame is a mixed blessing for them all. My brother is a builder now and he's funny about what it's like being a Barlow in Frodsham. 'Sometimes I think it's done me a lorra good. People might want me to build their house because they want to know a little bit more about Our Gary. But then you get the others that are right bastards. In a small town, of course now and again you're going to get mithered [that's northern for bothered]. Usually it's people going, "Oh, I went to school at the same time as Gary."'

Our Ian's got his favourite comeback: 'Oh, what time's that then? Ten to nine in the morning?'

I've sometimes thought about moving abroad. The thing about the UK is that in a London winter it gets light around 8am and then dark around 4pm. When I have told friends in LA that's what the days are like they say, 'WHAT! You choose to live there?' And the winters are getting harder.

So many friends have moved out to little villages lately, thinking life's better in the country. If I were to move out now, I reckon I'd last two or three years tops. I'd never judge other people's choices but the small-town life can be suffocating. In London there are theatres, museums, restaurants, bars, there's music and arts. And when you get ancient, there's lots of hospitals!

The older you get, I reckon, the nearer to people you want to be. What makes a city is the people. I need people. People are clever and inspiring, they fill me with ideas, and the problem with small towns is there's just not enough of them.

The other crucial thing with London is I have immediate access to everything. If someone calls and says, 'Write me a theme tune,' as they did the other night, I've got access to every musician, producer and editor in the world. The city is a corridor to the world. I love a city, I always dreamed of being a part of one. That's why I spent my childhood staring at the M56 – it went to bigger places.

But much as I love London life these days, I am proud that I was raised in a small town where I was deeply loved and supported by my parents. I'm from Frodsham and nothing will change that. Those are my roots, that is the soil little seedling Gary grew in. I was brought up there and it shaped me. It gave me the security and the self-belief to push on out into the world.

Not all kids gaze longingly at the horizon, at motorways and ports, or talk about capital cities, and dream of blue skies and America. I did.

# JUBILEE '77

*Music; it made things better.*

To get a grip on the Silver Jubilee let's just remember the times we lived in back in 1977. Those were long-face days, remember? Saying things like 'me time' was unheard of. Me time? Just get on with things and keep your mouth shut. 'My happy place'? No one felt they had the right to be happy in the seventies, you kept your feelings to yourself. 'Feelings' was a song by Morris Albert, but that didn't mean anyone showed them.

Life was different then. Any link to divorce meant complete shame, for the whole family. A divorcee was a failure. *What will the neighbours think?*

We still lived with a quiet threat of nuclear war – we forget how growing up we had that hovering over us. Raymond Briggs, creator of the ultimate warm Christmassy feelings generator, *The Snowman*, even wrote a colourfully bleak graphic novel about it, *When the Wind Blows*.

Strikes, the double whammy of inflation and unemployment – 'stagflation'. . . Hardly anyone had money back then, or, to be more accurate, hardly anyone had any access to credit. Life was a slog and that was normal.

We didn't eat out as kids and my parents didn't really drink. Men drank beers (about 20p a pint), and the wine glasses were tiny – a good thing, really – like little egg cups compared to the goldfish bowls we swill out of nowadays.

Obviously I was completely unaware of all of this, but I think as a kid I just absorbed a lot of repression and misery that was fairly normal in the seventies, and even at 6 years old I was subconsciously aware of it.

To top all this, Elvis is about to die.

Welcome to 1977.

People needed cheering up.

But then a Jubilee came along.

Us kids made paper crowns at school, and the streets were all jolly with bunting. But what really sticks in my memory is that I'd never seen people let their hair down before.

The guy in the bowler hat was Arthur Langwin, a big round-faced character. The Langwin family kept themselves to themselves. They had a caravan that never moved from its spot parked outside the front of their house, where it blocked all the light to their front room. Lovely.

Anyway, I'd never seen Mr Langwin smile in my life, or talk to anyone. Jubilee comes along and he's in a bloody bowler, cheerily hanging with all the kids in our street, including me in my smart double-denim ensemble.

Grumpy gits that hated their wives and kids and usually went out of their way to avoid going home, guys who spent most of their lives working, were suddenly all up and dancing and having a cracking time. The weather was quite extreme that year, there'd been a drought, all the grass was dry, scratchy and brown, and the sun was interspersed with howling winds (so British). Still, the grown-ups were laughing and chatting with each other in their best flares and wonky paper crowns.

All the nanas were out in their smart coats and the hats they wore to church. I watched all this in pure amazement and I loved it. I LOVED IT. I love happiness, love seeing people having a great time, and maybe that is the reason the Jubilee is etched on my memory.

As I've got older I've realised the Queen is genuinely worthy of our respect. The dedication, sacrifice, the nobility, stoicism, kindness and the quiet wit – she's incredible. But even the Queen isn't as good as music, is she?

Yes, the Jubilee was all about the Queen, but what drove the happiness of the whole event for me was music. Boney M, Status Quo, David Soul. Remember David Soul? Hutch to Starsky and absolutely huge in '77 – 'Don't Give Up on Us', 'Let's Have a Quiet Night In', 'Silver Lady', which I'm 99 per cent certain isn't about the Queen on her twenty-fifth anniversary on the throne but I can't say for certain. Wings' 'Mull of Kintyre' was huge, and Showaddywaddy – who were absolutely massive despite being essentially a massive covers band with colourful Teddy boy suits and brothel creepers. And Abba, of course. Mum said, 'Things changed when Abba came along. They brought music back.' 'Dancing Queen' was very popular at our house.

That Jubilee was an incredibly impactful moment in my early life because it showed me how music can change a person's emotions. How it can lift them up, or crystallise how they are feeling (because as we now know, humans do have feelings, quite a lot of them in fact, and it's OK to show them).

# BMX

*Dear Santa, please can I have plastic wheels for my BMX?*

The underlying love, as always with me, is people. With any pastime you come to realise that the activity itself wasn't the thing you *really* enjoyed, it was the people you enjoyed it with that counted the most.

My old Frodsham BMX gang were Hitch, Quinny, Molly, Bellie and me. When we all got BMX bikes we spent more time just sat on them talking than actually riding them.

We spent so much time together, the bond we had was special; my little gang was like a secret society and those days before girlfriends, exams, work, kids, all the grown-up shit, were magical times. Mars bar, can of Coke, bag of chips, we'd be out all day (see seventies style parenting).

We'd go scrambling up Frodsham Hill too, like the original Californian kids who took their normal road bikes in 1971 and rode them on adult motocross courses. The fad took off to such an extent that the bikes were modified so that they became like pedal-powered motocross bikes.

It was a trend started by kids who were just, as we say in the north, 'playing out'. And now, adults ride them at the Olympics. In 2003 it became an Olympic sport, and first appeared at Beijing in 2008. Incredible really, to make that leap.

I'm a person that gets into things – once I'd found a hobby, I wanted to spend all my time on it. I was a black belt at karate. And I loved my BMX. Mum and Dad used to take me up to Southport where they had a proper BMX track, which was next level, it had the ramps, the racing circuit. You'd see bikes of all shapes and sizes, and all sorts of skills. The big thing there was to grab 'air'.

You'd see lots of Mongooses in Southport. David Attenborough would have loved it. The Mongoose was the cream of BMXs. It was a piece of art. It was so simple – like a Tesla, pure, less is more – chrome frame, red crash pads and these flashy plastic bloody wheels.

The finishing touch was a race plate. Even better, an actual number on it.

The 'Goose was a top-shelf bike. The other out-of-reach brands were Diamondback and Kuwaharas, which was the brand ET chose to take Elliot for a ride on.

A BMX was designed to be ridden standing in your pedals, and for doing stunts and tricks: bunny hops, kick turns, aerials, tail whips, foot jams and, of course, wheelies. We did wheelies down Ship Street because it was long and straight. I think I managed 1,000m once. We had such a purpose when we were out there.

Part of learning anything is the crashes and falls. On a keyboard, these hurt your ears (see 'Whiter Shade of Pale'), in a career, they knacker your confidence, but on a BMX the wipeouts were epic – knees, elbows and sometimes your head. Those wipeouts were all part of the gig. Isn't that life? Nothing ventured, nothing gained?

BMX was really big, even in sleepy Frodsham. It was so major that Raleigh stopped making the mighty Chopper – remember them? – the bike of the seventies, the one with the funny seat and the gear knob on the crossbar.

Most of us Frodsham kids rode the Raleigh Burner, the Nottingham-made answer to the BMXs from California. People occasionally dared suggest to me that the Raleigh Burner was a second-division BMX and I'd feel the hurtful burn you only get when someone insults someone you love.

Most kids in Frodsham had a BMX. But not many had a 'Goose, which was the McLaren of BMX. When you saw one, you'd say something, or whistle. WOW! A Mongoose.

Funny thing is, though, in the great tradition of 'all the gear no idea', it was the kids with rubbish BMXs that could do all the tricks. The Raleigh got you some places, it was a good bike, reliable. I had two brothers for five years, Ian, and the Burner.

But it was the wheels I pined for. My Raleigh had metal spokes. The Mongoose had plastic ones. Plastic ones were the holy grail, there was a mythology around them. Plastic wheels meant you did better tricks; they were tough, if it bent it was said you could straighten them out in the freezer. Even today, you don't find them on eBay, they're collectors' items. They were a thing of beauty, them plastic wheels. I wanted some so badly.

I used to dream of those wheels as a kid, but at 8 or 9 they were out of reach. There wasn't a mortgage or a bank loan or paper round I could do to make those wheels mine. There was no instant gratification back then. I just had to wait 'til Christmas . . . and hope.

I only ever had the one BMX. I changed the brakes and got these fancy ones that stuck in the air, and pimped it constantly. I asked for them for a few birthdays and then finally, Christmas 1981, my mum and dad asked, 'What do you want, your yellow plastic wheels or a new keyboard?'

# TOTP: IT'S THURSDAY, IT'S 7PM, IT'S . . .

*All these guys had were keyboards . . . they were black. They were shiny. They were PLASTIC!*

'Pop of the Tops' we used to call it, entirely affectionately of course. Affection meaning holy worship. It was looking into a whole other world that was untouchable to kids like us in a small town. Imagine being on that show. The audience throbbed round every artist, all packed together, swaying, great dancers, flicking their big hair. It looked like a party.

And it always required sitting down waiting for the continuity announcer to say, 'It's Thursday, it's seven o'clock, it's *Top of the Pops*.' I'd shout to my brother, probably in synchronicity with five million other kids sat on sofas from the Isle of Skye to the Isles of Scilly, 'It's starting!!!'

Cue perfectly calibrated clapping, cheering and whooping, and the latest flashy neon camera effects. Oh, wow, the screen just exploded and reformed in the shape of loads of saxophones. And look at the audience, there's loads of them.

For me, the golden era in my memory was the period with all those New Romantics and electronic acts, Human League, Duran Duran, OMD (Orchestral Manoeuvres in the Dark), Erasure. And WHAM! The men were beautiful in the eighties. I wanted to look like them, have hair like them and sway side to side with the human hand claps perfectly synchronised with the sampled ones.

I was watching Depeche Mode in 1981 when something like a fire was lit in me. A light went on and a lot of others went out. I stopped thinking about yellow plastic BMX wheels. Seeing them perform their singles 'New Life' and 'Just Can't Get Enough' set me off on a pretty single focus. I wanted a proper keyboard. It was like they were a whole band of keyboard players with fantastic hair, Depeche Mode.

Think back to when Boy George was first on, that would have been the first time any of us small-town squares would have seen anything that culturally subversive ever. Is it a lady or a man? We had no idea, we lived in a world of blokes who wore trousers and long faces.

*Top of the Pops* was a horizon. It showed kids there was another world out there. There was no number 22 bus at the bottom of the road that went to 'Another world' or 'Out there'. *Top of the Pops* was our only window on it. It was like looking into a parallel universe. Everyone looked glossy and untouchable and incredibly cool. It was just like, Imagine being on that show. IMAGINE BEING ON *TOP OF THE POPS*.

How did you get there?

When Boy George was first on with Culture Club in 1982 we talked about it for weeks in the playground. Who on earth was this extravagant character who had suddenly burst onto the scene? Pop music brought a much bigger world into our small town.

My first pop fascination was Adam & the Ants. My curiosity kicked in when they had their first huge hit with 'Antmusic'. He was just breathtaking, such an original style, original music, mad, catchy hooks in the chorus. Nine-year-old Gary from Frodsham was even more glued to the telly when Adam Ant was on *Top of the Pops*.

More. I needed to know and hear more. I bought *Look In* magazine from the grumps at the corner shop up the road because Adam Ant was on the cover. This became my first delve into an artist. I was only young and Adam & the Ants were modestly subversive post-punk figures, but Little Gary had seen them on *Top of the Pops* and he went off into Chester with his mum and spent his pocket money on their first album, which had come out in 1979 and hadn't done well. It was called *Dirk Wears White Sox* – what a great name for an album.

I listened, and understood why it hadn't been popular. The music was much more jarring and punky and there were less drums. By the time I was into them, they had two drummers.

Their new sound, however, the sound I liked, was getting them on *Top of the Pops*. I was devoted all the way through 1980 and 1981, 'Stand and Deliver', 'Prince Charming' . . . then came 'Ant Rap', which finished me off.

I was ready for Gary Numan by then.

I always watched *TotP* with Our Ian and we had very different tastes in music. He hated Gary Numan. But that was the quiet subversion of Pop of the Tops, the incredible diversity.

When Take That started doing *Top of the Pops* (first time, 4 June 1992) we would be sandwiched between some rave act and soul singer or Lionel Richie and the Utah Saints.

Looking back, from a position of quite a segmented music market, I think this is wonderful. But at the time it was a different matter. It was a lesson in how fast pop music moves. As soon as we'd finished playing it was on to the next one. 'Well, that was Take That, and now . . .'

Hold on a minute, I thought it was all about us?! Was I disappointed? You bet!

It's a great leveller, *Top of the Pops*.

It was actually devised back in the early sixties as competition for *Ready Steady Go!*, which was a short-lived but briefly very influential music show on the only other channel on British telly at that time. Two channels: imagine that, kids.

*TotP* outlived the ITV show and ran from 1 January 1964 to 30 July 2006. Take That appeared on sixty-six of *TotP*'s 2,300 episodes and presented the 1994 Christmas show, which was still a big deal back then – no one had any choice what they watched on Christmas Day and only about four people in Britain had satellite TV.

It was a tiny studio, with the same audience members being herded around and told exactly when to go wild. No presenter in sight, they'd be down to film the links later. It was a bit of an anticlimax but it was still *Top of the Pops*, small studio or not, and we were on it because we were in the charts and that felt special. Now, when I'm working on telly, I always insist on every shot having loads of audience in it, because that's what looked magic on *Top of the Pops*.

Apparently, the star bar backstage was the setting for countless dramatic piss-ups, rock star wobblies and pop meltdowns – all these bands, bored shitless, knowing they've got to get up and mime, would drink too much and create a scene. But in all that time we as a band never got up to any mischief. That wasn't us.

Nigel, our manager, always had a bit of extra joy tacked on the end of any gig and we'd be rushed straight off to do an interview with a Japanese telly programme, or a magazine, or to catch a plane to Germany for an appearance. We never got to stop and have a drink with the other bands and appreciate where we were or who we were sharing the studio with.

Sometimes that makes me feel a bit sad, really.

For a while the producers were really into 'Live link-ups by satellite'. I remember doing a 'satellite link' from NYC, Times Square, because Nigel was obsessed with the whole brand message in a 'sat link' – he thought it made us look international. Honestly, I can't be certain, but I am pretty sure we just flew to New York to do *TotP* and then flew home. I think it was 'Love Ain't Here Anymore', and Simon Bates interviewing us. We definitely didn't have any business in the US, we were just there to look big. Managers are all about perception. Call me an old cynic, but I'm telling you stuff like that still definitely happens, they just hide it better these days.

When I put myself back in the head of that kid sat next to his brother on the couch, totally on the edge of his seat, squabbling about whether 'this one' is 'rubbish' or 'brilliant', I think, this is why I wanted to get into music. *Top of the Pops* was the centre of the pop music industry, it was the benchmark. If you were on *TotP*, you were doing OK.

And being introduced as the number one record this week . . .

Wooooooooaaaaaaaaaah. Fucking hell. This is it!!!

Watching *Top of the Pops* was a major part of being a kid, and an experience most British children shared until the nineties when it moved to a Friday night slot. By then the Internet was doing for it anyway, its place at the epicentre of pop music culture diminishing as the worldwide web expanded.

Why would *TotP* survive in an age when we have access to music by just shouting at Alexa or picking up our headphones? Back then, getting access to pop music required a ride into town on the bus to buy records, or cassettes, or waiting for your fortnightly fix from a music paper, or *Smash Hits*, or listening to a lot of Radio 1.

Over the years you meet people that knock it, but if you say, 'Really?', they always crumble and admit that yes, it was the lodestar of their childhood too. That's the thing, everyone watched it. I heard about a guy who knew a girl who knew a bloke who had a cousin that once met someone who watched the *Six Million Dollar Man* over on ITV at that time but I can't be sure it's true. I suspect it's an urban myth.

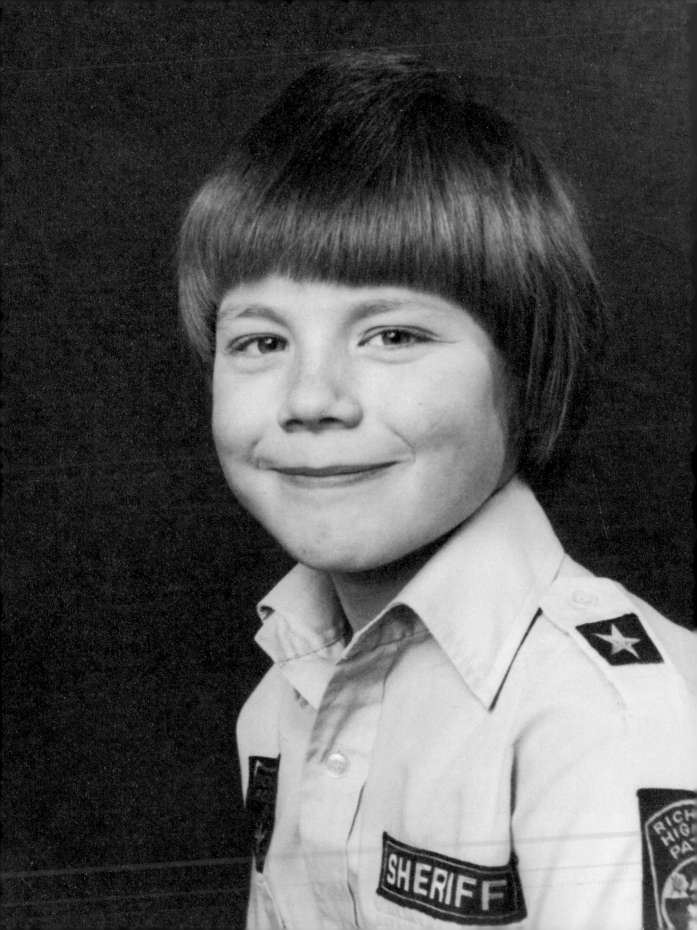

# CHIPS WITH EVERYTHING

*If you half closed y'r eyes at about 6 o'clock it kinda looked like CHiPs.*

When I wasn't out on my bike with the gang I would take my beloved pick 'n' mix up to Frodsham Park to gaze at the exciting skyline of Ellesmere Chemical Plant, or up to the rocks on Frodsham Hill, where I could look out across the promising vista that was the local motorway. I used to spend hours staring at that view. I was certain that that magical road led to something exciting, probably inspired by my favourite TV show of the time, *CHiPs*. Two highway patrol motorcycle officers in California find themselves at the scenes of copious multi-car pile-ups in the course of their thrilling crime-fighting action-packed lives.

Despite the crime epidemic on the highways, these dudes had plenty of laughs and we often saw the dazzling white teeth of Ponch (Erik Estrada – the really handsome mischievous one) and Jon (Larry Wilcox – more of a homely kind of good looking).

Through six series and 139 episodes, and never without their Ray-Ban Aviators, Ponch and Jon ride cool Kawasaki bikes pimped out with saddle bags, police radios, massive aerials and loads of lights.

To top off this kid-pleasing recipe, *CHiPs* featured those really blue Californian skies that seemed to characterise the world beyond the chemical plant, down the M56 and across the sea to *America*. AMERICA! (See also *Hart 2 Hart*, *Fantasy Island*, *Knight Rider*, *The Love Boat* and anything with the words 'Aaron Spelling Productions' in the credits.)

What perhaps made me fall in love with *CHiPs* so hard, though, was that it had a *really* funky theme tune written by an absolute legend called John Parker, who also did the music for many other shows, including the mighty *M*A*S*H* and *Dallas*. The *CHiPs* tune has a fat disco beat with dance-floor strings to match and special squelchy spaceship sound effects that would make Giorgio Moroder weep. This was a theme tune so epic it could have been played at Studio 54. But Ashton Drive had those funky beats pumping out of its tellies on a Saturday afternoon, just after tea time.

# THE GREBO

*Two lines of rockers, Our Ian in the middle.*

While my life was filled with riding my bike, imagining a life beyond the Ellesmere Chemical Plant, making my way through those weekly bags of pick 'n' mix and music creeping in and beginning to take a hold of my heart, I couldn't figure out what my brother was up to in his spare time. One night I followed Our Ian to the town hall. I knew that's where he sometimes disappeared to and I wanted to know what it was that he did in there. I was 9 or 10 and he was 13, so we were a world apart in child years.

When I got to the hall it felt really adult, it smelt of boys and sebum, it smelt of the teenage human male. It was a level beyond anything I could understand.

I think the DJ had a leather rocker jacket on, like everyone else on the dance floor. Some of the jackets had tassels on the arms, fringing. In numbers it looked like an army. I stood on my tiptoes and peeped through the window and I could see them lined up, all lads, with their legs wide (akimbo!), hands through the belt loops in their jeans. They would lean forwards from the hip and twist to the right, twice. Then repeat to the left.

After a couple more songs with them doing this, all the heavy metal lads went back and leant against the wall and all the mods got on the dance floor to Madness. It was 1981 and their album *7* had just come out – it was before they were massively popular, and were still seen as a ska/mod act.

The night from then on flip-flopped between the mods and the rockers. Mods and rockers had been famously at war for a couple of decades; scraps between youth subcultures were something to do at a time when there were no screens and only one or two TV shows aimed at young people.

Famously, over the Whitsun bank holiday in 1964 there were these great battles across the seaside towns of the south-east like Brighton, Southend and Margate. Fights between mods and rockers were tribal, traditional almost, I think a few may even have happened at my school. Or was that the skinheads versus the punks, of which we had about two? Like most small towns in Britain, our mild-mannered punks got the blame for most of the trouble in our town.

Our Ian made a good fist of making trouble too. Trouble, that's rebellion, it's a thing that separates you from the generation above.

But tonight in Frodsham Town Hall it all went off peacefully and any animosity was friendly and theatrical.

Ian went off every summer to see all these bands live at Donnington Park. Inside this world, he made all his best friends.

I don't know whether I would ever have gone on to join a youth culture tribe like Our Ian did. He was much more into the listening and the culture of music. He had all them black band T-shirts that would probably be collector's items now. Music is such a crucial part of those young tribes, isn't it? It sets you apart from your parents, from your kid brother.

It's like my son Dan now, with hip hop, it feels like stuff there's no way on earth your mum and dad would like. That's part of the appeal. Finding your own tastes, that's the start of growing up.

They might cut the umbilical cord at birth, but for years you're still just an extension of your parents. Other things will follow and mark you out as a different person with your own tastes. A few years on, Ian's love of music was swapped for a passion for Manchester United and that became the language between him and his mates, but to start with it was always music. Music is how you start to define who you are.

## 'SMOKE ON THE WATER' BY DEEP PURPLE

*Disco . . . Our Ian? Nah!*

Our Ian was a rocker to his core. He only ever played heavy metal, and he played it all day. His room was lined with all his vinyls. Led Zeppelin, AC/DC, Meatloaf, Axe Attack and, of course, Deep Purple.

Ian loved Deep Purple, he worshipped the lead singer, Ian Gillan. He was so into this music, he really listened, whereas I was always playing.

As soon as he woke up he put on Black Sabbath's 'Paranoid' or Motörhead's 'Ace of Spades'. I mean, how did anyone come up with a song like that? It's so fast. I suspect that doing the Grebo to Motörhead was quite a challenge, whereas 'Smoke on the Water' has a slow, steady tempo that would be good to steadily rehearse your Grebo moves to.

When I listened to his heavy metal through the walls of the Barlow family bungalow, with that bass so heavy it made the air shake, I didn't dare ever enjoy it. It was *his* music.

Forty years on, I listen to it now and I hear it as music, not as a statement. I can really appreciate those singers in a way I couldn't back then. They were incredible. High tenors, with these very soulful, bluesy voices.

That voice was there in all the rock of the seventies and eighties, right through 'til the mid-late eighties when the poodle-haired bands like Aerosmith and Whitesnake raised the pitch a bit.

This was a whole new style of rock, it's like all that hairspray seemed to alter their vocal chords. David Coverdale had been in Deep Purple in the seventies and went on to form Whitesnake – he went from this masculine baritone to this melodramatic higher pitch.

All those hair bands were about something much more identifiably Hollywood, whereas heavy metal was born down the M6 in Birmingham, with Led Zeppelin, Black Sabbath, Judas Priest. It was influenced by the blues from Black America, yes, but heavy metal was born in sixties industrial Brum.

I mean, I really do appreciate the history now, the artistry and the music, but it was impossible back then because, you see, you've got to play these records loud and Our Ian's sat there in his room with his head between the speakers enjoying the hi-fidelity effect, but for the rest of us it was always too loud and a major pain in the arse.

With these songs, you're not just listening to a voice, or a sound, it's a whole performance. These bands were recording their songs in one take. They'd rehearse for weeks and then record it live in a studio. So what you've got here is some seriously great artists playing.

That lead singer might be a great guitarist, a great singer, and then there's the performance up on the stage where they could carry it all. They had performance drummers.

These bands, they'd have been friends since school, they were more than a band, they were a gang, a collective voice.

There's not a lot of musicians capable of that these days. Those songs weren't angry, punk was angry, these metal songs were earthed and grounded. Just look at the poetic lyrics of a song like 'Smoke on the Water'.

You've got to respect them. Most of these guys were pissed and off their heads a lot of the time. I don't really know a lot about that place where drugs and music meet, never been my thing. But I know a lot of those guys were probably on acid, their minds were in some seriously altered states.

Even if you can't see the artistry in the music, you've got to have a bit of respect for how the fuck they were coming up with, recording and performing this stuff in that state!

# 'WHITER SHADE OF PALE' BY PROCOL HARUM

*Suddenly I've got a much bigger organ.*

It was early summer 1983 and I'd managed to steer my dad into Rushworth and Dreaper in Chester, a branch of the famous Liverpool organ makers.

Rushworth's had been making and selling church organs since about 1840. We didn't go for those though, we went past the organs proudly displayed at the front of the store, to the modern section, Rushworth's Music House, where they sold all the electronic organs, and the guitars, and this stuff called 'video' equipment. Basically anything that relied on electricity was considered dead modern. The Beatles had gone to Rushworth's in Liverpool to buy their first Gibson guitars.

It's an historic company and it was a sort of Mecca for me because it had everything I wanted. If you were into music, you went to Rushworth's, for anything from a grand piano to a 7-inch single.

In the eighties Rushworth's was flying high, it had three branches in Chester alone. The one we went to was down at the bottom of the city by the clock tower. Rushworth's went bust in 2002, it failed to move with the times, and all the wonderful stuff that filled its five floors in Liverpool, four in Chester, can be found inside a laptop now, inside a phone even. So sad, the columned palace where I bought all my early equipment is a Ladbrokes bookies now.

Back then, though, the A55N was the first time these *electronic* organs had been sold at an entry-level price of a few hundred quid. Still a lot of money back then, but Japanese Yamaha brought electronic music to the masses in a way American brands like Hammond and Wurlitzer couldn't, or wouldn't. Their organs, like the one played on Procol Harum's original version of 'Whiter Shade of Pale', cost thousands, even back then. A little kid like me couldn't even dream of ever touching one of those.

A Whiter Shade of Pale
Words and Music by Keith Reid
and Gary Brooker
Slowly (♩= 76)
Organ
mp

# ELECTRONIC ORGANIST

Gary *BARLOW*

Frodsham

Tel:- 33657

Now, these electronic organs were a real craze back then. Compared to nowadays' kit they're like wind-up gramophones with a bloody great trumpet on top, but back then they were the cutting edge for your living room. My first business cards proudly announced, 'Gary Barlow, Electronic Organist', which sounds ridiculous but was actually a fairly handy job back then because with an electronic organ you could bring all these transistorised sounds to your set. You were a one-man electronic orchestra.

Yamaha knew what my dad would learn that day at Rushworth's. You sell someone something really basic like the PS2 and they're gonna need to upgrade sooner or later if they don't pack it in and take up the next big craze, like Swingball or Rubik's Cube.

I needed a new keyboard. My mum said, 'You outgrew your keyboards faster than your trousers at that stage. You had the small Yamaha for Christmas and had grown out of it by Easter.' But it was several weeks' salary and the Barlows had no spare cash. So my dad, my bloody amazing, quiet, stoic, grafting dad, decided to sell all his holiday back to the fertiliser factory where he worked and spend £399 on the A55N Yamaha.

The sheet music for Procol Harum's 'Whiter Shade of Pale' came in the box.

The song spent six weeks as the UK's number one in 1967 and went back into the top ten again in 1972. However, I discovered one of the most played songs of all time (according to BBC Radio 2) in 1983 when I sat down at my shiny new organ.

The song has this whirling, swirling classical organ as its main feature, which is famously inspired by Bach. Some say it's a direct copy of Johann Sebastian's original but those claims are incorrect on a technical point. You can't actually copyright chords or bass movements, only melody and lyrics.

The Bach reference appears in what is called the 'descending bass' part and mastering that is how I learned to use the bass pedals on my A55N Yamaha organ. You start at the top and descend through the notes, pressing your feet. It is a brilliant way to learn.

Procol Harum's 'Whiter Shade of Pale' was my organ teacher.

It is one of the biggest-selling singles and most-played records of all time and from the outset it's something of an enigma. The lyrics weave a moody story of love and loss with this big soul vocal against a classical organ background. It's quite unlike anything else out there.

Everyone else asked, 'What does it mean, to "Skip the light fandango"?'

Me, I was getting to grips with sheet music and my A55N Yamaha organ and at the age of 12 all I wanted was to master the organ part. It required a combination of playing melody with your right hand, chords with your left and a bass line with your left foot while controlling the volume with your right foot.

It was not easy. But I can't describe how completely obsessed and focused I was on getting to grips with it. The minute I pressed that first key on the Yamaha that I got Christmas 1981, it wasn't natural, or gentle – I was possessed.

It's like rubbing your belly, patting your head and tap-dancing all at the same time. It took six months to actually get it to feel natural, and I spent most of the time looking at my feet. Which is why I can play without looking at my hands.

Progress was slow, baby steps. Those six months were painful and frustrating for me. But imagine how it was for Mum, Dad, Our Ian. The poor neighbour, no wonder he always looked so grumpy.

But I got there. This thing wasn't going to beat me.

Malcolm Gladwell wrote in his famous book, *Outliers*: 'Ten thousand hours is the magic number of greatness.' He believed that to be considered an expert at anything you must practise it for ten thousand hours. Forget talent, you don't become amazing at anything overnight, it takes years and years of practice. (And deafening your family.)

It takes time.

The recording of 'Whiter Shade' features the Hammond organ that's kept by Abbey Road Studios, which has gone on to become one of my favourite places on earth.

The Abbey Road Hammond has been there since 1967. I've often sat down to play it, it crops up a lot on *The Circus*, but never a feature like 'Whiter Shade'. Nothing can compete with that.

The lyricist was Keith Reid, an unusual band member in that he didn't sing or play an instrument, he just wrote very unfathomable words. He was quite young when he wrote 'Whiter Shade'.

I read an interview he'd done in *Uncut* magazine where he said, 'I had the phrase "a whiter shade of pale", that was a start, and I knew it was a song. It's like a jigsaw where you've got one piece, then you make up all the others to fit it. I was trying to conjure a mood as much as tell a straightforward, girl-leaves-boy story. I was trying to be evocative. I suppose it seems like a decadent scene I'm describing. But I was far too young to have experienced any decadence, then.'

I get that – my early songs were all about my ideas of the adult themes that generally appear in most pop songs, like love, heartbreak, sex (see 'A Million Love Songs', page 72). Whereas now I write from experience about all sorts of things, not just the obvious pop themes.

# WORKING MEN'S CLUBS

*'Lad, I think you've got potential. Would you like a gig?'*

I got my first gig as the resident Saturday-night organist at Connah's Quay in Wales. (Yes, I had an international career from the get-go.) Mum and Dad would drive me over and wait and drive me back. They'd do this pretty much every weekend for the next five years until I learned to drive.

Connah's Quay was my first gig. It was in a working men's club. Often the default is for people to take the piss out of these places but I've always been very clear about the role they played in my early years as a musician. I daresay I take the piss myself. It's what we do with so much of our working-class heritage in this country, especially from the south and looking north.

If you hear the words 'working men's clubs' and only think of old fellas with broad northern accents talking about whippets, there's much more to these places. They've been the heart of working-class communities since Victorian times.

The first working men's clubs were opened by a teetotal Protestant clergyman called Henry Solly who wanted to replicate the upper-class gentlemen's clubs of St James's in London and provide the working men of the industrial north with somewhere to go that was more educational, affordable and sober than the pub.

Solly's intentions were noble, and the number of clubs grew in industrial areas across Britain, but the no-drinking rule didn't last long. Unsurprising, that. I also played in Labour clubs and Conservative clubs, which were the same sort of thing, clubs owned by the members for the members, with cheap beer, entertainment, and the pub sports of dominoes, darts and snooker. Maybe a football and a cricket team.

Whether it was their work, or political beliefs or, in the case of the British Legion, time in the armed forces that united them, to me it never felt like anyone was into much more than the beer and the company. On some nights they'd 'bring the missus and kids out'. And then they'd want bingo or whist and a dance at the end of the night. Those were the nights I played.

I often laugh about me setting up my keyboard in between the real main events, which included the hot meat pies arriving, gruffly announced over the club intercom with the word 'piesvarrived'. But sometimes it really was like that. 'Piesvarrived' could mean my entire audience got up and left. I'd be upstaged by meat and gravy in pastry. Then there was the bingo, and the meat raffle. (Literally, a raffle with meat as prizes.)

# CONNAH'S QUAY LABOUR CLUB

## Saturday, 7th April, 8.00 pm

# D'ARMOUR

Great top class duo Plus

## SKY HIGH DISCO

*Teenager "GARY" on the organ in the bar Come and hear young talent.*

D/AW1

Greenall Whitley Weekly News
CLUB ACT of the YEAR

Pearl

NO SMOKING

**Halton Royal
British Legion**
Main Street
Runcorn
☎ **Runcorn 64860**
**Members Notice**

Friday, June 23
**AVALON**
*Fabulous duo*

Saturday, June 24
**SUNSET SOUND**
*Group*

Sunday, June 25
Lunchtime:
**HAL NOLAN**
*Top TV comic*
Evening:
**GARYS FAREWELL**

**Tote Nos 10 + 34**

Playing these clubs, I wasn't hanging out with people my own age. The compere, the drummer, the bass player, the other acts, they were all adults that had done things and been places. They spoke this whole other language and, as a teenager, I felt very shy around them. I had to be able to speak to them. In some ways, I was raised by wolves. I'd sit in those smoky clubs, chatting, gigging, jamming. These were my friends, I didn't know any musicians at school.

I was popular at school but my head was always somewhere else. This kid I was at school with told my mum this story about him once running into the music room one break or lunch or something. I was practising on a keyboard and he said, 'Gary, you've got to come and play football. We need you.' I was quite good at football, and there was one of those break-time matches going on that all the pretty girls were watching. 'Gary, you've got to come, we have to win.'

'No, I've got to practise,' I said.

The kid said to me, 'Come and play football, you'll never get any girls playing that thing.' I didn't go.

When I was 14, I became the resident keyboard player at Halton Royal British Legion. It was a big deal. Saturday nights at these places, the big buffet spread is out, the bingo cards are on sale, there's pictures of the Queen, Princess Diana and old Armistice Day parades around the walls. The kids are in the pool room, the more committed drinkers in the bar, which has a dartboard and is away from the distracting noise of the entertainment. Outside the Gents, with the gentlemanly wafts of urinal cakes and urine, are the fruit machines. A military type will come out and shout the winning bingo card numbers. Mum and Dad always sat in the same place, towards the back of the room. Dad, like Our Ian, trying to avoid talking to anyone. If people came over to ask him a question he'd just refer them on to Marjorie, to my mum (the boss).

I think, if I'm honest, I was a bit of a novelty because I was good. When I left Halton, Ken Dodd's music director replaced me and swapped my 4/4 time modern stuff for 3/4 waltzes and 2/4 marches. It never really mattered who you played or how well you played it though. You could very rarely play so well that the woman who always seemed to be screaming and cackling at the back would shut up.

Take That are famous for their shows. It's a big show, Take That. I reckon part of the reason our shows are so dramatic was in an attempt to get that woman at the back who'd rather play bingo to sit up and get involved. I always wanted people who came to our shows to feel so immersed that they forgot about everything else that was on their mind for an hour or two.

I started at Halton in 1985 and Chris Harrison started as the compere in 1986. I remember him saying to me, 'I can see you performing in front of thousands one day.'

Bless him. He had a never-ending stream of one liners – he still does, he's still there.

Chris still goes for tea occasionally at my mum's, she's stayed in touch with him. He's a lovely guy. He'll tell you that tea at my mum's is shocking, 'I got an electric shock off the currants.'

There were thousands of performers going through these clubs and we all had these dodgy agents that did fuck all and took 15 per cent of everything. You'd get a call: 'Right, lad, Goose Green Labour Club want you Thursday night.' There was no contract, your contract was your name on a whiteboard in the foyer advertising your forthcoming appearance.

The basic process of becoming a singer or a musician starts off with bedroom rehearsals and then eventually you find an audience. As you get tens, then hundreds of gigs under your belt, it gives you an education and experience that can't be taught, it comes from countless hours in front of audiences. Malcolm Gladwell's ten thousand hours.

Artists can't be made in a moment. My mum saw The Beatles in the early days in Liverpool at The Cavern, when they were still just doing cover versions. That's what they did in Hamburg for two years in the early sixties, sleeping in concrete store rooms backstage next to the club's toilets. You do what you have to do when you are still learning about yourself, or in a band when you are learning how to be a single unit that can think and work together really instinctively.

When I got home after a gig, I'd plug my headphones into my DX7 keyboard and play in my bedroom 'til four.

By the time I joined Take That I had done thousands of gigs. The only people that have that level of experience these days are buskers, like Ed Sheeran was. I don't know if the sort of experience I got exists now. There aren't the same kinds of live venues, there aren't the same audiences. It's hard to imagine how the working men's clubs will survive the next fifty years with all the booze and entertainment you could possibly want delivered to your door and on a screen at home.

I might take the piss with the 'piesvarrived' banter, but that doesn't negate the education I received from the clubs. By the end, I had a proper agent and I had a backing band (more proper grown-ups).

When I was playing these places in the eighties they were an important circuit for a lot of entertainers. For some they were the *only* circuit. That's certainly how I felt.

What was known as the Northern Club Circuit had some very big venues, like the Halton Royal British Legion.

Here, and at other big venues like the Montrose in Liverpool, I was performing to an audience that had seen them all. They were big tough rooms, crowds there had seen some huge comedians and musicians because those bigger clubs had the capacity to attract big stars.

During my time spent playing the working men's clubs, I went from playing in my school uniform to my final gig with a trendy haircut and Simon Le Bon-wannabe pegged trousers. Within a year I'd have a proper manager and a band made up of kids my own age.

## MUM AND DAD

*Mum and Dad, grinning ear to ear.*

I'd leave the house after breakfast – aged 9 – and with a quick look back my mum would say, 'Make sure you're back before it's dark.'

That was standard back then.

We were left to our own devices because there wasn't much choice, there were no devices.

We never sat in the house. Everything I played with until the keyboards arrived was about being outside. Telly was rationed. By then there were three channels, then in time, four. But that new one was very racy. We didn't have much. It wasn't a middle-class world we lived in, it was all the different shades of working class.

My parents weren't really big pub-goers, but I've got so many friends that have a golden kind of nostalgia about long summer evenings when they were left in a pub garden or locked in a car with a bag of crisps and a soggy paper straw stuck in a warm bottle of lemonade pop. (We weren't allowed that 'American crap' Coca-Cola in its cool curvy bottle, even though it was all we really pined for.) Meanwhile, the grown-ups got stuck in at the boozer. I mean, people don't even leave their dogs in the car these days.

Was it child abuse or just a perfectly practical solution to childcare while Mum and Dad had a night out? The Coke and crisps were cheaper than a babysitter.

For better or worse, kids were exposed to way more risks back then.

More kids ended up in hospital (or worse) due to accidents and falls back in the good old bad old days.

But that had nothing to do with Marj and Colin being somehow inadequate. My mum and dad were brilliant. People just did things differently then.

Seat belts? Mum used to say, 'Ooh, I don't like seat belts, they make me feel claustrophobic.' Don't like your tea? Eat it up or you won't leave the table. Parents work all day? That's OK, the kids already walk to and from school.

We were left alone to make our entertainment. Childhood was a mix of freedom and periods of great boredom. These days kids never get bored, they've got movies, games, Netflix, social media . . .

I don't know necessarily that one childhood trumps another. What's important is that kids feel loved, but there is a danger that nowadays they are so constantly entertained, and so safe, they never find that curiosity and confidence that we had to dig deeper into passions and hobbies.

The crucial question is, would I have played 'Whiter Shade of Pale' quite so much on my new A55N Yamaha through summer 1983 if I'd had YouTube to keep me amused all day and parents fussing over me, taking me to pottery-painting classes and tennis lessons?

My parents were selfless. They never did anything except focus on what was best for their kids. Mum and Dad married in January 1967, and Our Ian came pretty swiftly after, then me, the greedy-for-attention kid. Dad worked. Sometimes two jobs. He only really started

being around when we moved house in my early teens and I think they had a bit more money. But at the weekend, he was always there when I was playing in the clubs. However many gigs, three or four usually, him and Mum would settle at the back, orange juice for Mum, lager and lime for Dad, and watch.

I know I have made my parents really proud and we have all enjoyed my success, but they've also had their fair share of the bad bits that fame can bring. Like Mark's mum and dad too, they had the journalists going through the bins looking for anything they could build a story around. The band and I would just get on a plane and go to Japan, but all the parents were left at home with kids scribbling messages all over their houses. Mum's never complained though. 'Oh, we just got on with it, they were mostly pretty harmless. It was quite nice in a way.'

They let me make mistakes. If I played a set that was too long, or a song that didn't work, they never said anything and just let me work it out for myself.

What I got was really good parenting. It's why Gary Barlow isn't Sid Vicious. I was safe, I was loved, I was supported. As a parent, I can see that now and I am so grateful.

A member of the pathological staff at Bootle General Hospital, Miss Marjorie Cowan, daughter of Mrs. Cowan, of 31 Wilberforce Road, Walton, married Mr. Colin Barlow, son of Mr. and Mrs. Barlow, of 8 Clifton Crescent, Frodsham, at Walton Parish Church, on Saturday. Given away by her uncle the bride wore a classic gown of white satin with a shoulder-length veil and rose head-dress. She was attended by the bridegroom's sister, Miss Sandra Barlow, and the best man was Mr. Kenneth Nield.

[Photo by J. Baron Williams, Great Crosby.

> Put your head
> against my life, What do you hear?
>
> A million words just trying to make
> The love song of the year.

## 'A MILLION LOVE SONGS'

*'I like that one, who's it by again?'*

I was tinkering about with songwriting and would play my own stuff in among the cover versions I'd be learning for any gigs that week. My bedroom was too full of kit for Mum to sit in there while I was playing but she'd pull up a chair outside and give me her opinion.

I must have been playing 'A Million Love Songs' a fair bit and one day she asked me who had written it. Me, I wrote it, Mum.

People wonder how I wrote an evergreen love song despite being a teenager. I was 15, same age as Lorde when she wrote 'Royals'. Billie Eilish wrote 'Ocean Eyes' when she was 13. I'm not sure musicians decide what to do when they're in the careers centre at sixth form, it takes over your life young. I only had eyes for music.

I'd not fallen in love yet. I had a long-term girlfriend throughout secondary school, Heather, and perhaps an idea of what love might be. But while I inhabited an adult world and could talk to old fellas in the working men's clubs, the R in Gary didn't stand for romance.

Keith Reid wrote the surreal and psychedelic-sounding 'Whiter Shade of Pale' at the grand age of 19 and admitted he cribbed the weird psychedelic atmosphere in the lyric from books and films.

It was the same for me. When you write young, it's creative but also a process of regurgitation. It's like you put a load of songs that you love in a mental blender with the goal of writing a ballad, a sweet love song – Neil Diamond's 'Love on the Rocks', 'Stuck on You' and 'Hello' by Lionel Richie, and I was mad about A-Ha at the time – whizz it in your mind and out comes 'A Million Love Songs'.

It's not about copying. I loved these songs so much, they were in my DNA. In the act of writing you add something pure and sincere of yourself. 'A Million Love Songs' is beautifully innocent and extremely simple. A good idea is a good idea, doesn't matter when you come up with it.

*Close your eyes, but don't forget*
*What you have heard*
*A man who's trying to say three words*
*The words that make me scared.*

'A Million Love Songs' is written in a 12/8 rhythm, like the Righteous Brothers' 'Unchained Melody', like The Animals' 'House of the Rising Sun', like Tears for Fears' 'Rule the World'. It's in the key of C, which is my gateway – more about that later.

'A Million Love Songs' wasn't written with a band in mind. It is extremely simple, it's just four basic major chords and a guy sat at a piano singing D E F G, a range that is the sweet spot for my voice.

I was proficient in keys quite early on. I know how to play a song in any key, I can transpose any song to a whole new set of notes. For years I'd got used to accompanying other singers in the clubs, male and occasionally female, crooners, balladeers, even borderline operatic, all sorts of artists. It was clear to me early on why songs were in a certain range. By the time I opened my mouth to sing publicly aged 15, I knew a lot about music.

My writing relies on my voice; having a good singing voice makes it easier to write because you don't build these songs note by note like they're made of Lego. It's always about a feeling. The songs started, and they still do, with the performance, the voice, the song, the melody – not being written down on a manuscript or on a step sequencer.

I write with my hands and my voice first. Always have, always will.

I first performed 'Million' in the working men's clubs. I asked the compere if it'd be OK, blew on the mike and let Halton British Legion have it. They liked it.

Seven years later Take That recorded this song and three others that were on the tape I had given our manager Nigel Martin-Smith when I first went to meet him at his office in Manchester. Another one was 'Nobody Else' – I wrote that after school in my bedroom at home too – and we didn't release that song 'til 1995, the best part of a decade later.

I've always been good at cataloguing my ideas. The newest idea is always the shiniest but I never just discard them. I've got files and files of work going back nearly four decades.

When it comes to a time to write an album, no one sits down and knocks it out from scratch. When I was writing *Open Road* in 1997, I was sometimes tinkering with melodies and ideas from when I was still at school.

As the nineties progressed my music got more autobiographical, and by the time we got to 'Never Forget' in 1996 there was a glimpse of something more lyrically meaningful.

'Million' was my first hit record. It got to number seven in October 1992. With it I got a taste of what it is to write, record, and then perform your work on TV.

Wow! So that's how it feels.

Once I'd tasted that, it made me want to write more. It was just the beginning.

God bless Bob, what a guy.

One thing he always said was,
'You've got to get out of those clubs.'

# BOB HOWES, 'A SONG FOR CHRISTMAS' AND TIM FIRTH

*By chance, by accident, by HOMEWORK . . . I'd written a song.*

Bob Howes is a classically trained musician, a band leader, a choirmaster, a creator, a businessman and an academic. He is a genuinely multitalented man, what they call a polymath. Bob first introduced the 'A Song for Christmas' competition to the BBC in 1976.

The junior songwriting competition was on *Pebble Mill at One*, which was a daytime telly institution that was filmed at the BBC's studios in Birmingham. Bob was the producer. The competition was mostly for choirs, but over the twenty-six years it ran they let a few solo entrants in. A solo male had won the year before I entered.

My music teacher, Mrs Nelson (Val to her friends), set us songwriting homework and encouraged me to enter Bob's competition. When I made it through to the final rounds she chaperoned me to Birmingham for filming. I don't know who was more thrilled, me or her. Probably me, but it was close.

A few other teachers and people from the town came up to be in the audience. Me being on telly was a big moment for a small town like Frodsham.

Aged 15, with three and a half years in the clubs under my belt, 'A Song for Christmas' was a big step up from Halton British Legion.

Bob Howes had an assistant, a student at Cambridge University called Tim Firth. Tim had entered 'A Song for Christmas' as a kid and Bob had stayed in touch with him. Bob was great like that. Bob himself had won his first singing festival when he was 7. Bob, Tim and me were very different in age, in background, but we shared an all-consuming passion for music.

I didn't know this at the time, but that wasn't the only thing we had in common. Tim was also from Frodsham. We took the train back up there together after the recording and have been friends ever since, nearly forty years.

Back in 1986 you couldn't just 'be on the telly'. You had to *do* something. It was a competition but for schoolkids, it was lovely. You weren't voting for the personality or the carefully constructed sob story. You just voted for the song they had written.

We performed in the studio's outside courtyard, the quadrangle, which was smothered in artificial snow and the BBC's entire annual fairy light budget. Christmas trees everywhere. 'Let's Pray for Christmas', my ballad parading as a carol, went up in the semi-final against a more traditional Celtic carol written by a Welsh schoolgirl and her choir of twelve girls.

There was no one close to me, I thought. The choir was vanilla, their carol predictable, whereas I threw everything I had at this song, pulled out all the tricks: a key change chorus like Barry Manilow would do if he wrote a Christmas carol for the Copa, like 'After the Love Has Gone' by Earth Wind and Fire, like 'This Time I Know It's for Real' by Donna Summer. A chorus key change really puts your song on a pedestal.

And that's not all. I also had a sax solo, like 'Careless Whisper' by George Michael, like Gerry Rafferty's 'Baker Street'. And the lyrics, they had everything – Jesus, tinsel, snow, Bethlehem, love – they were all the Christmas songs I'd ever heard put in a blender.

I didn't win. Carolyn Hitt's Celtic carol did.

Carolyn's written before that I said to her, when I lost, 'Well done, something good will come out of this for all of us.' I'm glad I gave the impression of being a sporting loser because inside I was bloody furious.

For a few years after that Bob Howes was my mentor – he's a beautiful man, a gorgeous, caring, talented character. He was the first person involved in television I'd ever met and was everything you could hope he'd be: warm, talked nicely to everyone, firm, clear, well-spoken, and in charge.

I'd go to see him at his studios every four months. A studio, in London! Just arriving at London Euston was like rocket fuel to my ambition.

God bless Bob, what a guy. He was the first person I met who had 'meetings'. The phones were always ringing but when I came down to visit he'd switch every one off and properly listen. He'd send me his thoughts on my songs in this wispy, intellectual handwriting that looked to me like it had been written with quill and ink.

Even as I started to get famous, he gave his time selflessly and had zero interest in capitalising on me financially at a stage in my life when I found more and more people wanted something from me.

And he pushed me. He'd say read this poetry, listen to this classical piece, look at these lyrics. With my own lyrics he'd urge me on to rewrite and rewrite until the lyric was in its simplest yet most sophisticated form.

One thing he always said was, 'You've got to get out of those clubs.' He thought belting out tunes night after night was turning me into a crooner, 'Too much vibrato, Gary! Neil Diamond? He's not in the charts any more.'

He pushed me to do better, always.

Now that's a mentor.

And I met Tim, we went home together to Frodsham on the train and I wrote my number in his Filofax. He was wearing a white coat, sort of like a cross between Dr Frankenstein and Doctor Who. I think it's the sort of thing people who join the Cambridge Footlights wear. We were very different, but that's OK, I was good with different. I sent him a little cassette of four of my pop songs.

As Tim remembers it, 'There you were, this kid from Frodsham in your pink woolly Christmas number with your angelic pink cheeks, and then you opened your mouth to sing and out came this rich, mature man's voice.'

Tim admitted to me only recently that as soon as I finished singing 'Let's Pray for Christmas', him and Bob had turned to each other and said, 'We've got to stop him reaching for the stars.'

Well, it was far too late for that. There's absolutely no doubt that as well as being into music, writing, singing, performing, listening, and ambitious to succeed, I also just wanted 'to be on the telly'. I was obsessed by music but also I was determined not to have a real job.

To do all this without fame, what was the point? I value the performing, I like being an entertainer.

'A Song for Christmas' was my first glimpse of the big time and I loved it, all the fuss, all the cameras pointing at me. To be in a recording studio, and to record with all these musicians behind a massive microphone in front of a massive mixing desk. I wanted it all again.

I still love it today.

Oh yes, I had stars in my eyes.

# BLACKPOOL

*Gary Barlow, opening act, Talk of the Coast 1988 in Blackpool.*

'Clickety click, sixty-six. Legs eleven, eleven.'

I can hear the bingo caller fade in and out as I pass the Mecca. There's pop music coming from the amusement arcade, along with the dings, rings and racket of the slots. 'Agadoo, do do, push pineapple, shake the tree . . .', daft song, but Black Lace's 1984 hit was still going down a storm in Blackpool in the summer of '88. Their other hit, 1983's 'Superman', still gets lots of plays here too, as does that classic piece of diabolical pop, 'The Birdie Song' (1981) by The Tweets. Welcome to Blackpool!

I walk on. 'Agadoo' is swapped, thank God, for Gary Numan's synths in 'Cars'. I like that one. Walking on, beery, faggy smells and Status Quo leak through the doors of a boozer. Ding, ding, ding, a shower of change rattles down. Someone just won on the fruity.

All this to an aromatic back beat of salt, vinegar, and the fish that swim with a battered sausage. On, past the Imperial Hotel, where I hear a snatch of a string quartet accompanying the tea dancers.

That was the soundtrack of my early-evening commute along the Promenade from my B&B (breakfast strictly at 7.30am, not 7.29, or 7.31) to work at The Talk of the Coast at the Viking Hotel.

I remember telling Mum, 'Hey, Mum, I've got a summer season at Blackpool.'

'Blackpool! Gary. Blackpool.'

We were still in that era where to play in Blackpool meant you were at the top of your game. People forget that after London, Blackpool was the biggest showtown in the country. In this respect it was like Vegas, or to put it more correctly, Vegas was like Blackpool, which has got a century on the flash arriviste in the Nevada Desert.

Four nights a week, summer season 1988, June to September. Monday through to Thursday. In Blackpool they get audiences on nights like that, because people are on holiday. They're packed out.

I've been sniggered at over the years because of my links with Blackpool. Do I care? No, I don't. Sod 'em. Snobs! That place was my university. Blackpool made me never take an audience for granted and always give them a show.

Blackpool has been a showtown from the moment it was born. It was purposefully built up from four villages by a handful of Victorian families in the entertainment business. When Walt Disney was preparing to build the first Disneyland he came to Blackpool with all his senior guys for advice and inspiration. It's true!

There are these big leisure clubs, pleasure domes, like the mid-nineteenth-century Winter Gardens. The Blackpool Tower opened in 1894 a week before the Manchester Ship Canal. Manchester was one of the most important cities in the world then. The first industrial city *in the world* in fact. It deserved the bright lights of Blackpool where the Tower's ballroom outdid Versailles for opulence. Gilt-edged? It's gilt *everything*. The floor alone is majestic, made up of over 30,000 pieces of oak, walnut and mahogany. Unlike Versailles, it had, still has, a circus underneath.

My friend Amanda Thompson is the great-granddaughter of one of those Victorian founders. She runs the Pleasure Beach – again, one of the first amusement parks in the world – that her family founded 125 years ago. Amanda remembers the animals from the circus being exercised on the beach. Forget donkeys, 'You'd see the elephants playing in the sea.'

Incredible. Gives me goosebumps. The history made in that town is just incomprehensible.

Let's not get too teary-eyed, though, some of the venues in Blackpool were horrible despite being loaded with history. I've long wanted to make a TV show about the North Pier. It's just a rickety looking clapperboard box built in 1863 in the grey Irish Sea on the Lancashire coast, but the people that have played there would blow your mind.

Later came places like the Mecca, which looked like a multistorey car park, all pebbledash, grey and grim, but nonetheless similarly important and historic. The Mecca's Highland Rooms was the heart of the Northern Soul scene, with all these pasty white northern kids swivelling, shuffling and swan-diving to uptempo Motown in a club their nanas might have done the foxtrot in earlier on at tea time. Ballroom dancing runs through this town like its name runs through a stick of rock.

Everyone dances here. Every other building's a dance school. Even the girls on the lash, shivering in the queue for the nightclubs – with their big coats left at home on a brash February Friday night – will be up on that podium.

Meanwhile, downstairs, the Mecca had the country's biggest snooker hall – twenty-five tables. The Commonwealth Sporting Club always had a famous player in there practising, often with a pint. It's not that I'm a snooker fan, it's just the way it sat cheek by jowl with the Blackpool Symphony Orchestra at the Winter Gardens.

Don't forget the comedy. Blackpool doesn't have a Walk of Fame like Hollywood (a lesser-known showtown in some place called California), but it has the 'Blackpool Comedy Carpet' underneath the Blackpool Tower. Where else can you walk on 850 jokes?

It was comedians I was supporting at The Talk of the Coast. Suddenly, I'm sharing a bill with these huge stars. On a normal night, there'd have been Stan Boardman, Ken Dodd, Bob Monkhouse, Cannon and Ball, Bernard Manning . . . I'd be supporting three a night at The Talk of the Coast. People loved these classic eighties comedians and Saturday night schedules on the telly were built around them. They were big stars.

I loved music, I didn't want to be a comedian, but at this stage the big musicians were miles away from me as a performer. I was nowhere near Duran Duran. I was never going to share a bill with Dire Straits. But these comedians were right there in front of me. I'd play 7 'til 7.30 and then go straight into the audience night after night to watch these guys getting the reaction I craved: a standing ovation.

I used to watch those standing ovations thinking, How can I get one of them? You've got to be good, but to get the applause, you need to take the audience on a well-planned journey with you – you need to have a show graph.

I've never grown out of the place. I've turned on the Blackpool Illuminations twice. Once in 1995 and once in 2013 when I stepped in and switched them on when some band dropped out. I'm not proud, anything for Blackpool – even second billing. I did the Royal Variety there in 2020, and the following summer I took Our Daisy up there with her gang of friends from school.

All the seaside towns in Britain were for middle-class and upper-class people until a railway was built linking the coast with some of the Lancashire mill towns in the mid-nineteenth century. This meant the working classes could get there easily, cheaply and en masse. Blackpool station had fourteen platforms, more than London Paddington.

Back then, the working classes didn't really get holidays. The odd religious festival was your lot, now get back out there and

work 'til you drop dead, and that applies to the wife and kiddies too.

All they had was something called Wakes Week. The Wakes' origins were religious but by the Industrial Revolution they were actually used so the mill owners could fix up their machinery for a week. The workers in the cotton mills formed clubs where they saved a little all year to have enough money for their one week of unpaid holiday (paid holidays didn't come in for nearly another century, ditto the luxury of a weekend).

The combination of savings clubs and the laying of railway to the coast meant the factory workers could all afford to take breaks in seaside towns during the Wakes. You've been toiling six days a week in a noisy Lancashire mill all year round and then you go off together with your co-workers, friends and family to the gilded ballrooms, the ghost train, the big dipper and a boarding house probably not that dissimilar to the one I sometimes stayed at. Can you imagine the excitement?

Some factory workers throughout the north and Scotland still got their Wakes Weeks right up to the 1980s. The Glaswegians even kindly brought their own police with them to Blackpool for theirs.

Never was there a point with Daisy and her mates that I needed to explain it to them. They might be privileged west London kids but what they loved the most came for free, all the colourful lights on the trams.

Blackpool had some of the first-ever electric street lights in Britain in 1879. Street lights were an attraction in themselves back then, but by 1912 the town had upgraded these to something a bit more twinkly, the Blackpool Illuminations. Can't have a showtown without lights. Coming to see 'The Lights' helped stretch the summer season's end in September through to the brash and bracing reality of November. It's one of my earliest and happiest memories of childhood, driving to the coast to see them.

Being able to create light and magic and 'artificial sunshine' is very necessary on the Irish Sea coast in November, even now. Imagine how dazzling that must have been in the forties and fifties when, as we know, everyone lived in black and white.

The brighter the lights, the darker the shade. Blackpool has light and shade in massive doses. It's not like Disney World where everything's very precisely sanitised and stinks of cookie dough, where you don't see the messier side of existence. You just see the costumes

and then when they're not smiling they go down a hole and disappear. I struggle to think of a big British seaside town that doesn't have that eerie mix of joy and gloom.

The weather was great when we went with Daisy and I said to her, 'I don't think I've ever been to Blackpool and seen the sun shine.'

Our kids have always been to Blackpool. They love the whole rigmarole of the drive up. First to spot the Tower gets an ice cream. The rides, the lights, the shows, the chips.

We were on a plane off on some exotic holiday once and I said, 'Right, kids, of all the places we've been, where's your favourite? Marks out of 10. Hawaii?' 'Eight!' 'Australia?' 'Six.' 'Barbados?' 'Seven.' 'Blackpool?' 'Ten!' All those fancy holidays. Wasted. There's nowhere like it in the world.

You get a great audience there, they just give and give. No one's there by accident in the way they might be in London or the smart cities. I'll admit, sometimes I walk that seafront with my brolly up thinking, 'Mmmn, this could be a grim show.'

It never is.

# THE SHOW GRAPH
*. . . the first ever GARY BARLOW SHOW GRAPH.*

On the nights when there was a second act playing after me, I'd sit at the bar and watch and try to work it out. The other acts weren't better than me, they just put the songs in a different order.

There were other things I spotted, like the 'money note'. In movies, the money shot is a scene that is a huge audience pleaser. The money note is a long dramatic note at the end of a song, and the audience can't help themselves, they love it. Like Pavarotti singing that long B 'Vincerò!' at the end of 'Nessun Dorma'. Anything by Celine Dion – she is a walking, talking lyric soprano money-note cashpoint. When she hits and holds the high note in 'My Heart Will Go On', it doesn't matter if you hate the song, you cannot fail to be moved.

The show graph is about experience. Audiences are not predictable, you have to adapt to survive. I needed to learn how to get an audience from nought to sixty night after night. I needed to become a good entertainer. You had to think on your feet or you wouldn't get a clap. Not one. And I hated that. It'd ruin the whole night and I'd drive home depressed.

I'd arrive, set up, and in the first five minutes on stage I had to read the place. Sometimes you'd have a young crowd, meaning about 45, other times they were really quite elderly, in which case you did a sedate set, and turned the volume down a bit.

It was essential to get them all singing, maybe clapping their hands. Give them a gap in the music to join in. You needed to make friends, by walking into the crowd with your microphone, singing to individuals, perhaps a little playful teasing. I was jotting it all down in my mental notepad and these tools I learned in the working men's clubs became my first show graph.

You've got to think of it like a movie. Things happen, there's jeopardy, drama, highs and lows. The songs are in an order and they tell you a story. It goes a little something like this . . .

### 'The Phantom of the Opera' by Andrew Lloyd Webber

*Show 'em what I can do.*

The song from *Phantom* is all about showing them what I can do. 'Oooh, look at this kid, he can sing.'

The original cast recording of Lloyd Webber's smash musical spent nearly three years in the UK charts. The title track, with Sarah Brightman and Steve Harley singing their 'strange duet' between the beauty and the beast in the story, spent a few weeks in the top forty around about the time I added it to my show graph. Coincidence?

## 'Sweet Caroline' by Neil Diamond
*Time to make friends with the crowd.*

The music grabs them, and then you go walking out into the crowd, making friends.

Neil Diamond's 'Sweet Caroline' has a verse-to-chorus build with the force of a tsunami, it gets any audience swaying, singing, on their feet and covered in goosebumps. It is a force of nature.

It came out before I was born, in 1969, but didn't reach its highest UK chart position until I was likely sitting in my high chair in the summer of 1971, throwing baby food at the radio as it played Radio Merseyside.

I bloody love this song. I'm in good company because it's been covered by loads of people including Frank Sinatra, Elvis Presley, Roy Orbison, Andy Williams and Bobby Womack – blimey – and, from the sublime to the ridiculous, Dustin the Turkey. Yet it's never been number one anywhere in the world. Just goes to show, the greatest songs don't necessarily get to number one. It's in C major. Mmm, my favourite. What's not to love?

## 'The Power of Love' by Jennifer Rush
*It's time to get emotional.*

Everyone loved this song at the time, but it's a ladies' song. What am I doing singing it? Well, there's a lot about these clubs that's done with a wink of the eye and they loved the knowing way I changed the lyrics.

Celine Dion is better remembered for it now, but Jennifer Rush, with her enormous opera-trained voice and matching hair, will always own this song for me. Her version came out in 1985 and was the biggest-selling single that year. In fact it was the biggest-selling song ever by a female solo artist in the UK until 1992, when Whitney Houston monstered the charts with 'I Will Always Love You'.

It's also got a huge long money note. All in, a sure route to a standing ovation – and especially on the more abandoned nights of the week, Wednesday to Saturday.

## 'Copacabana' by Barry Manilow

*Start the big build to the end.*

'Copa. Copacabanaaaaaaah.'

This song is a rocket. It packs so much in, it's dazzling. Musically there's this great late-seventies disco groove, which is not a genre known for its storytelling lyrics. Storytelling is Country and Western, less so pop. In pop it's rare.

Lyrically, it's a story song about murder, jealousy and alcoholism, yet it is also funny. At one point the backing singers' refrain is 'have a banana'.

In just two verses 'Copacabana' manages to tell an epic tale of a club where a dancer, Lola, falls in love with a guy, Tony, who after a shoot-out with a love rival, Rico, either dies or goes to prison for life.

Our Lola ends up at the bar of the same club, one verse and thirty years later, in her tattered old showgirl clothes drinking herself to death.

It's just bloody astounding. It's like a whole Vegas show wrapped up in four minutes. It's a pina colada for the ears, hearing it makes you feel like you're on holiday, it makes you want to dance. Imagine me dropping that at Connah's Quay on a rainy November night. 'Copacabana' is the key to a door. It lifts the audience up, literally.

It's like 'Relight My Fire', it always gets them out of their seats. It puts everyone on a high.

Barry Manilow is a good friend of mine now. He is one of the geekiest guys I know – just wants to talk about chords all night, which is my idea of heaven. In my experience, anyone who is passionate about something, anyone who is good at what they do, they are always seriously a geek. People talk about Keith Richards as this great wild rock 'n' roll figure, but the truth is, you get him on to guitars and he'll be a geek, just like Barry and me.

### 'The Final Countdown' by Europe

*He can play this fella an' all.*

Three words: *iconic keyboard riff.* And I played it on a keytar. That's right, a light keyboard that hung round your neck like a guitar.

The song itself is an absolute classic of Swedish soft rock, some distance from the heavy rock I grew up listening to through the walls of Our Ian's bedroom. There are plenty of great piano riffs in pop, Abba, Elton, Kate Bush, Joy Division (I can just imagine that going down a storm at the Halton British Legion), but they'd sound a bit odd on a key-tar.

'The Final Countdown' helped me feel like Howard Jones and Nick Kershaw, the synth pop heroes I worshipped via *Top of the Pops*.

Apparently it was inspired by David Bowie's 'Space Oddity', which just goes to show how far the space can be between influence and composition.

It was number one in twenty-five countries. Number one here in late 1986. It was massive but wasn't often performed on 'the circuit'. While I'm singing the hot single of the year, the others settled on Dire Straits' 'Sultans of Swing' or a spot of Roy Orbison's 'Pretty Woman'.

### 'Celebration' by Kool & the Gang

*Black cycling shorts and a massive bomber jacket with some massive Fila trainers.*

This is a chance to dance and look like the people in the charts. I'd run off and give myself sixteen bars of drumbeats before a puff of smoke on my return, wearing cycling shorts, a funky bomber and a pair of red Filas. A bit of a foot shuffle, the running man, throw in a few eighties moves.

The Kool & the Gang guys killed it in the States with this song in 1980. The writer of the track, Ronald Bell, claims it was inspired by the Koran, somewhat ironic given it's a post-Disco stalwart of a million drunken wedding dance floors.

# THE FIRST TRENDY HAIRCUT

*Stage direction: Emerge with blond mullet wig.*

There was a girl called Christine Williamson in Our Ian's class who wanted to be a hairdresser. Her sister Denise had her own salon, Blondies, at the bottom of Ashton Drive. Christine wasn't old enough to do anything more than sweep up hair there on a Saturday.

She wanted to do more, and I was up for being her model. She nicked a rubber highlights cap from her sister and did my hair at youth club one night. I can't be certain, but I'm pretty sure I took an issue of *Smash Hits* in with a picture of Duran Duran for inspiration.

That youth club do was a dry run.

Between the New Year and my birthday in January 1990 I went back to Christine for more of the same, but this time a cut as well. I had two things on my mind – I wanted to look like Simon Le Bon, but even more, I wanted to get out of the clubs.

I'd had a really successful run of gigs round New Year. I'd been booked at the Leyland, a big place in St Helens, and it had gone so well the manager said as he counted out my money that night in the early hours of 1 January, 'Fantastic! I want to book you for the next New Year.'

It's a big deal in the clubs, to be booked for the biggest night of the year when it's still 365 days off.

But I said no. At an earlier gig something had happened that was a massive moment for me. There was a husband and wife act on the club circuit, they were musically pretty good but they sang covers – like most of us.

They were older, but then everyone on the club circuit was.

I'd asked them, 'Why do you still do it?'

'Well, you never know if he's out there.'

'Who?'

'Mickie Most, of course.'

Mickie Most was a sort of Simon Cowell who'd been a hot producer and then a telly talent scout in the seventies. They honestly thought that he was going to turn up in some northern working men's club and whip them straight down to London to cut an album at Abbey Road.

It was a bolt from the blue, visceral, I felt it in my body.

Jesus Christ. They're all dreaming of something that will never happen.

The next day I was straight into Blondies. They highlighted my hair and then cut it into a spiky top with a mane of hair to the shoulders behind, a sort of mullet really, but a very suave one. This magnificent do was all pop star. First division stuff.

I told the booker at the Leyland I wouldn't be working the clubs by 31 December 1990, so I couldn't take the job. He was flabbergasted.

The haircut was about a rebrand of myself to do what Bob Howes had been urging me to do since 1986. Get out. The decade had turned and so had I.

I'd go on to have many more pop-star haircuts, including a spiky platinum blond number that looked absolutely brilliant (I like to think) but also left me with scabs all over my head every time we did it. A pop star must suffer for his craft.

Denise still runs Blondies, and it's still there at the end of Ashton Drive, should you ever need your highlights doing.

# KNOW YOUR POWER POP HAIRDOS

## 01
## SYNTH POP PROTO-MULLET
Simon Le Bon, David Bowie,
Tony Hadley, Limahl, Cher, Paul King

## 02
## POST-PUNK POMPADOUR
Howard Jones, Billy Idol, Morrissey,
Thompson Twins

## 03
## WEDGE WITH A BIG FRINGE
Flock of Seagulls guy (Mike Score),
Phil Oakey, Gary Numan

## 04
## METAL HAIR
Long hair – like Lemmy from Motörhead, and pretty much every other metal band, and a teenage Ian Barlow – not to be confused with soft rock hair

## 05
## SOFT ROCK HAIR
Cleaner and bigger than metal hair, backcombed, teased, permed and, I'll be honest, wasn't big at my school – Europe, Whitesnake, Poison, Twisted Sister, Bon Jovi

## 06
## BUBBLY PERM
Which is subtly different to the female solo artist bubbly perm – Dolly Parton, Whitney Houston, Kylie, Sinitta, Cher, Deirdre Barlow

## 07
## MOD FEATHER CUT
Paul Weller, Rod Stewart, Nolan Sisters

## 08
## FLAT TOP
Kid 'n Play, Suggs from Madness

# NIGEL MARTIN-SMITH

*. . . it was like meeting Jesus.*

Nigel Martin-Smith was more of an agent when I first went to meet him at his office in Manchester. He'd worked with all sorts: models, comedians, actors, some singers. Behind his desk he had a disc, it looked lustrously gold around his head. At 19 years old that blew me away.

I'd contacted Nigel cold, the same way I'd go down to London on the train and wait in the lobby of record companies with the hopeless hope someone might come down and take a cassette of my songs from my actual hand. (They never did.)

New Kids on the Block were one of the first eighties American boybands who had made fortunes in records, tours and merchandise. Nigel was fascinated by the success of NKotB and he was not alone. Nigel was like Lou Pearlman, the guy who put together some of the biggest US boybands of the nineties (including the Backstreet Boys and NSYNC).

Lou Pearlman died in jail after effectively turning his bands into some kind of Ponzi scheme, so you could say that we were very lucky to have someone like Nigel. And for many years we were.

Nigel was invested in me as an artist from early on – he'd come to Talk of the Coast in Blackpool and unpack for me bit by bit what he liked, and what had to go.

Nigel took it upon himself to educate me.

'This is a Ford Escort XR3, Gary.'

'This is London.'

'This, Gary, is a hotel.'

'This road, Gary, this is Tottenham Court Road, there's a lot of music shops along here.'

'Gary, come to Florida, to a place called Miami.'

But he was also invested in Take That, I mean, quite literally invested, he mortgaged himself to the hilt to pay to get the band off the ground.

Nigel put together Take That and in the process he created the blueprint for boybands, which might explain why after we arrived on the scene the UK was suddenly awash with five lads, all slightly different, doing vocal harmonies, bopping about in an eye-pleasing formation and wearing carefully coordinated outfits.

You can thank Nige for that.

Where he really wrote the script was in the way he built us a presence and a fanbase. When we did a gig, and we did a lot in the early days, he had us run out throwing cards into the audience for them to fill out their names and addresses. His genius was accumulating the data on our audience. He'd direct mail them.

At first he was convinced we belonged in the gay clubs because that was where he was sure our audience was. We covered a Village People song at our first gig. But when Nigel saw the response at an under-18s disco in Hull he started targeting the young teen-girl audience too.

This took our schedule to a whole other level of madness. On a normal day we'd start with a gig in a school assembly. We'd run on stage at a school hall in Derby or wherever and it was just mayhem. The girls rushing at us, all grabbing and screaming, the lads all stood at the back scowling, going, Who are these boys with their tops off?

That over, we'd drive in the van to a school down the road to do a gig in morning break. What's weird at this stage in the very early nineties is that we were getting some magazine covers, so all the girls were going nuts and then coming over wanting us to sign their *Look In* or *My Guy*.

Next part of the day we'd do radio roadshows, shopping centre gigs, local radio interviews, then a quick dash back to our B&B to get ready for the evening. An under-18 event around 6pm, a club around 11 and then later in the night the gay clubs.

For a year we were gigging like this non-stop.

Gradually Nigel accumulated this information, so that in May 1992, when we released 'It Only Takes a Minute', a cover version of the old 1975 Tavares disco hit, Take That had a database – and potential fanbase – of half a million addresses.

Nigel Martin-Smith was at the cutting edge there. This is standard practice now. And it's much less labour-intensive because them algorithms can do all the heavy lifting. Our Nige, though, he was data mining when Mark Zuckerberg was still in nappies.

Once we started getting hits, the B&Bs turned into better and better hotels. We took nicer flights. At every level things became more comfortable, except one. The schedules remained packed, and in some ways it got worse because you're throwing in a ten-hour flight and a nine-hour time difference.

Things took off in Europe and Asia quite quickly, and if the labels there had paid for you to come over they would want to squeeze every drop of blood from you to get their money's worth. Straight off a flight to Tokyo, we'd be into a round of interviews. Days, weeks and months went by without a moment off.

At that point we were still grateful, still excited, and we would do anything for the label as they still had all the power.

When the second album did well, Nigel said, 'Hey, boys, I've got something to tell you – I've got all the power now.'

When Nigel was dictating things instead of the label we felt more protected, we weren't as battered and bossed about. We still grafted, but we knew then we were a precious asset.

Do I believe Nigel Martin-Smith is the reason I'm here? If he hadn't plucked me from obscurity would I still be on the Northern Circuit? It's a big question. But without doubt, in those early years he was magnificent.

We'd go on to travel the world, but very rarely with him. His assistant Ying would usually accompany us – he preferred to stay home in Manchester. And as we became more curious about the world he increasingly became this home bird. He just loves Manchester. He'd made so much money with Take That, yet he stayed with his lovely husband in the same house, with the broken handle on the toilet and a back door half off its hinges.

I don't know if he had a grand plan, he was learning as he went along, but he was clever, hard-working and observant. He was always watching like a hawk. But he was not experienced.

Do I believe Nigel Martin-Smith is the reason I'm here? If he hadn't plucked me from obscurity would I still be on the Northern Circuit?

It's a big question. But without doubt, in those early years he was magnificent.

That gold disc behind his desk (or was it silver, now I come to think of it?) was for a novelty artist called Damian's cover of 'The Time Warp', the cult song from the *Rocky Horror Show*. Damian's version had first emerged in Manchester's booming gay club scene in the mid-eighties, and Nigel had been trying to make it a hit for years in the eighties. He only got that gold halo once he got the British pop producer Pete Waterman to work on it.

What I'm saying is that what Nigel did was very smart, unique, I totally respect that. The big 'but' is that he felt to us five kids at the time like he knew what he was doing, but I think that he was actually a smart guy who was winging it, just like the rest of us.

Throughout the nineties, Nigel seemed to have a sixth sense about what we should be doing next. He hated everyone and constantly told us the record labels were useless. His constant mantra was, '*We* have to make it happen.'

I've never lost that very sensible suspicion of the machine that he instilled in us.

From the moment it began, we worked. I don't want to sound all Derek Zoolander, comparing the toil of modelling to coal mining here, but we took our working-class work ethic and applied it to becoming a great boyband. For five immature guys we were ambitious and we weren't scared to properly graft. I think a lot of bands get a bit of success and rest on their laurels. We just never stopped working.

We worked together and the combined might of us five under the strict control of Nigel was a winning one. We had the songs, too – as time went on, I knew what was needed of me and I wrote constantly.

Nigel and I have had our ups and downs. He played around with our heads, played divide and rule games. By the end of it we all called him 'The Manager' behind his back.

Robbie's never forgiven him, and our fans can be hard on Nigel for that reason. But Marjorie Barlow, who is kind, decent, fair and wise, she has a very soft spot for him. Mum won't have any of the nastiness. Mum's right, I'm forever indebted to Nigel for the springboard he gave me.

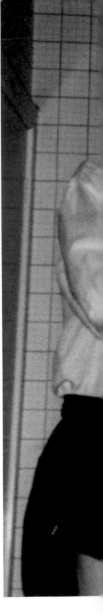

*Everyone brought something.*
*I wouldn't appreciate quite*
*how much they all brought*
*for some years.*

## TAKE THAT AUDITION

*'I wanna make Britain's answer to New Kids on the Block.'*

People assume that Nigel threw this huge audition and he had this carefully thought-through boyband shopping list. Right, they'll all be incredibly handsome, and fantastic dancers – one might even sing. I'll need a cute one, a dancer one, a funny one, a muscly one and a brainy one. The queues would be round the block, right? There'd be regional heats. In the movie of my life, I wish this was true.

The reality was that only six lads turned up to the 'nationwide audition' at La Cage nightclub (it was more of a wine bar really, but let's not rub the gilt off the moment any more than I already have). Only five of us made it simply because the sixth lad had way too much body hair and looked like he drove a taxi. He was too man for a boyband.

Nigel had already recruited me. I had the songs. At 19 I had the skillset and the mindset of a grown-up, I'd been performing since I was 11. During my years in the clubs I was hanging out with grown men in my backing band, dealing with club managers. I'm used to shaking hands.

Robert Williams was a pretty experienced performer too, he'd been in all these musicals, but he was so young, 16, he had to have his mum there. Howard Donald took a half day off his job as a vehicle spray painter; he was 22, the oldest, a part-time model and covered in paint from work.

The others all brought something crucial. Howard's modelling meant he could teach us all to look down a lens. Jason was 20, a dancer, he'd been on telly and he'd left home. Mark was 18, cute, adorable. All the teenage girls would love him. Everyone brought something. I wouldn't appreciate quite how much they all brought for some years.

Howard's modelling meant he could teach us all to look down a lens.

# 'DO WHAT U LIKE'

*Rolling around in ice cream and dairy whip stark bollock naked.*

I'd loved all that New Romantic, New Wave, synth pop stuff in the early eighties, but I didn't know anything about what was really contemporary. This was something the show graph couldn't teach me.

When I first met Nigel in 1989, I was writing songs like Neil Diamond in 1977. Now I'm in a band with four kids who want to be New Kids on the Block.

We were living in an era of a lot of dance music crossing over from the clubs. The dance music scene was having a massive influence on the mainstream and the charts were full of Madonna Vogueing, C+C Music Factory, Adamski, Deee-Lite's 'Groove is in the Heart'.

Add to that: Nigel was still convinced we were going to be a smash in the gay clubs.

You need to be able to actually dance your socks off in a club, not sway with a lighter in the air. I needed a bit of help here.

Nigel had been taking me to all these clubs; we were regulars at all the gay clubs on Manchester's Canal Street.

I was learning. He put me together to write with a guy called Ray Hedges. He played me a cult Chicago House track called 'Work it to the Bone', which features a simple tribal drumbeat that is perfect to dance to.

Ray and I wrote this crazy song, lyrically all about food, cherry pie, sugar sweet, jam. I still look at those lyrics and wonder where the fuck they came from. The whole thing, it just wasn't me.

RItZY

Weedon Road,
Northampton.
Tel: 0604 751351

T H E   T O U R

**TAKE THAT - LIVE**
**WED. 6th NOV. '91  7.30-10.00pm doors open 7pm'**
Admission: £2.50 (With this ticket)  £3.00 (Without)

# TAKE THAT

## THE BRAND
## NEW SINGLE
## "DO WHAT U LIKE"
### RELEASE DATE: 22 JULY, 1991
ON DANCE U.K. RECORDS
VIA TOTAL / BMG  CAT NO. DUK 02

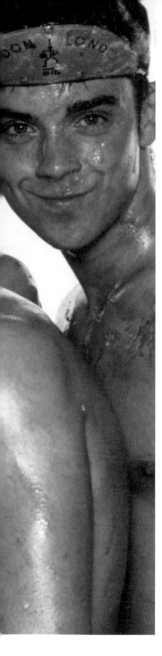

We wrote it, I sang it, recorded it, and then took it back to the van we travelled around in and played it to the lads. They loved it.

Nigel was convinced the way to get the attention on us, and to get a major label record deal, was to get the record banned. Well, that wasn't going to happen, the lyrics might have sounded a bit filthy but they were technically about bread and jam, it was hardly Frankie Goes to Hollywood's 'Relax'.

We needed not just to be heard but *seen* too. Time to shoot the video! Us in black leather, oiled up like five slippery eels, having a food fight with cream and jelly. They popped a few girls in, but it's clearly pitched at the gay market, which is still where Nigel thought we belonged. As Howard famously said, 'I was cleaning jelly out of me arsehole for the next two years.'

Still, even with all that and our naked backsides lined up like a bike rack as the lingering closing shot, *and* my incredible now platinum-blond hair, the song never made the charts, and by charts I mean the Top 100. It was Top of the Flops! We were banned, but only from daytime telly on the sensible old BBC. So, no appearances with Gordon the Gopher on *Going Live* but ITV had no problem with it.

I never played it to my mum, I could just imagine her going, 'Oh no, what are you writing this for, what's happened to all them lovely songs?'

When the band got back together in 2006 we went to the US to work with the hotshot producer John Shanks. The label had sold us as this great Brit band. We arrived. He clearly knew nothing about us so went straight onto YouTube and found 'Do What U Like', with its video of us rolling around in jelly and ice cream wearing our skimpy leather clobber.

We walked in and he was pointing at the screen saying, 'Oh man, this is crazy.' Inside he was thinking, Get these dickheads out of my studio.

'Do What U Like' went against my every instinct when I wrote it in 1991 and it was a lifetime away from who we were in John Shanks's Hollywood studio in 2006. But. BUT! Say what you want about 'Do What U Like', it got us signed by RCA Records.

# 'IT ONLY TAKES A MINUTE'

*Cue: Top of the Pops Theme!*

The story of this song starts with us all in a bit of a funk. And not in a good-time James Brown sort of a way.

We were trying loads of different stuff and hadn't left the studio for weeks. We'd do anything to find a hit.

Things had got so bad that we'd even asked the record label for advice. Never ask the label! We were panicking and there was no hiding it.

I first heard 'It Only Takes a Minute' while I was driving the van, I had it on cassette. It's a disco song by an act called Tavares. The original was far too high, of course – those tight disco trousers did something to men's voices in the seventies.

I played with the rhythm on my new sampler.

We were all excited about the producer, Nigel Wright, who was one of the founders of the jazz funk band Shakatak, who I loved right through the eighties. I used to play their stuff in the clubs.

We went to Chertsey where Nigel had his studio. We recorded it and it sounded like a hit. Straight away. We all knew. While Robbie did an ad lib, Howard and Jason were already working out dance moves.

Sounded like a hit, but how to make it one? This was our last go, we couldn't fail.

Two nights later we had it in the set list. Problem is, the label had had a load of staff changes and that's the worst, because all the new people lose interest in anyone they haven't actually signed. So Our Nigel drives down to London to collect the new marketing manager in his XR3 and drives him up to Nottingham to this place where the crowds always went totally mad and clawed you half to death.

It was chaos. And it worked. The marketing guy was completely sold and went scuttling back to London to tell all his colleagues they had to throw their weight behind us.

'It Only Takes a Minute' got to number seven in 1992. We performed on *TotP* for the first time. We'd done it.

We performed on TotP
for the first time.

TAKE THAT
It Only Takes A Minute

We'd done it.

> *Suddenly I'm not the kid from Frodsham, I'm the kid with a sampler.*

## A QUICK WORD ON SAMPLERS

*Bye bye, piano! This is the nineties in a box.*

For the last forty years samplers have been an integral part of music. Basically, a sampler allows you to record any sound and play it across the span of a keyboard – could be birds tweeting, doors closing . . . whatever it might be, it can become music. This gives endless possibilities in the way only machines can do.

Ray Hedges tipped me off about samplers when we were writing together. Nowadays everyone's got them on their laptops, but back then they were still a bit of *Tomorrow's World*.

There's a very famous sample of James Brown singing 'Hey!' taken from the track 'Funky President' that has been used countless times, especially in hip hop. What you have right there is a piece of the Godfather of Soul, delivered to your song at the press of a button. Who wouldn't want that!?

Ray showed me a sampler and I loved it. It just makes you go, Wow! That was the charts right there. It instantly made me look as good as everyone else in the band. Suddenly I'm not the kid from Frodsham, I'm the kid with a sampler. It instantly put me on a pedestal. But then you have a small problem. Now the tail's wagging the dog . . .

My songs were being written to it, they were servicing the machine. I was creating beats and baselines and then finding a fit for them. That's why the lyrics were so stupid at that time, I'd spend five hours making a snare drum sound and then write the lyrics in five minutes.

They just had to fit the latest miracle sound coming from the sampler. And mimic the whole New Jack Swing vibe which was about heavy synths and sampler sounds that added up to a very chart-friendly, poppy hybrid of hip hop and R&B.

'Sure so sure'. So not me. 'Holdin', squeezin', touchin', teasin'/Wantin', wishin', waitin', thinkin'.' So not me. It was all about being ghetto fabulous, which, you know, I really wasn't. Think about En Vogue's 'Hold On', Bobby Brown's 'My Prerogative' or 'I Wanna Sex You Up' by Color Me Badd.

It made me fit more into the band, that was the best thing. To see them shining bright to this music meant everything to me.

# 'RELIGHT MY FIRE'

*I've got hope in my soul.*

Now *this* is a show graph song. It gets them out of their seats and puts everyone on a high. With 'Relight', Take That's show starts to build. With 'Relight', my dreams were coming to life in a way I could never have imagined. Nigel's predictions were becoming reality.

It was written and originally sung by Dan Hartman, who was a musical genius. The Beethoven of Disco. He was like Prince, could play every instrument. Hartman wrote copious songs for other people. It was Hartman's songs that revived the career of the Godfather of Soul, James Brown. And then he released his own storming anthems of disco; more catchy than Covid, his songs are treasure.

I've got a good range in my voice but this Hartman sang high. When we recorded 'Relight' we had to take the key down a tone and a half for me. All the men sang so high in the seventies – the Bee Gees' falsetto voices were the tip of the high-tenor iceberg. It must have been all those tight trousers again.

When the DJ played a Dan Hartman disco track everyone would run to the dance floor. And that's the point of 'Relight my Fire'. It is a load of bloody fun, you can't help but dance and sing. It's a great song that lets everyone forget their worries. Job done!

The decision for us to cover 'Relight' was the work of Nigel at his gunslinging best in the early days when everything he did turned to gold. It's a helluva song.

It first came out in 1979, when disco was considered pretty toxic, very uncool, but then ten years on it was having a renaissance in the northern clubs, where DJs were mixing it into house music sets. One of the first DJs to do that was Joey Negro, who did a fantastic remix of our 'Relight'.

And then to bring Lulu in to sing the female part was one of Nigel's best moves. He had a thing about her.

Lulu meant something to Mum and Dad too. Mum was impressed. Lulu had been all over Radio Merseyside in the sixties and now here I was working with her. It was incredibly exciting. If I'm honest, pretty much everything that happened at that time was exciting, it was the start of something. Over the next two or so years we released nine singles, and only one, 'Love Ain't Here Anymore', didn't get to number one.

The charts don't mean much now. As kids they were a sort of North Star of pop that we all tuned in to, we all looked at to find out what record had sold the most that week. Today all that music culture is so scattered. Now, the charts include streaming, downloads, hardly any physical sales of CDs or the revived vinyl format. They are not the centre of the pop world. Most kids probably don't even know that charts exist.

Back then the charts were everything in pop music. In July '93, 'Pray' was number one. With 'Relight' we had our second number one a few months later, and then another, 'Babe'. It looked like that was going to be a Christmas number one but we were knocked off the top by a giant pink spotty foam creature called Mr Blobby. Showbiz, eh!

# 'BACK FOR GOOD'

*When you're a songwriter, you can't fake what makes your heart beat faster.*

I was in my house in Plumley in Cheshire when I wrote 'Back for Good'. It was my first mega house with a swimming pool and a big room that I converted into a studio.

The whole album, *Nobody Else*, was written there in a fortnight. We were in between a South Asian tour and a European tour, and the label said, 'We need the album. You've got two weeks.'

The rest of the band went off to Mykonos for a holiday and I went home and started writing. I'd wake up at midday or so, roll out of bed and straight down to the studio, and I'd be in there 'til I went to bed around five. That went on for years, that did. Years. Only kids would put paid to that habit.

I was working with a producer called Chris Porter on the album and he used to always comment on how beautifully I played piano. 'But I hardly play any more,' I said, 'I've got no time for a piano, I need to learn dance routines and try and get on top of my back flips. And anyway, I've got *a sampler*.'

It was Chris Porter, really, who encouraged me back to the piano, and sitting at its keys I wrote 'Back for Good'.

Chris said, 'Ignore all that shit, just play, just play your piano.' Because he used to compliment me all the time, I got back into playing. I needed that encouragement. Chris wasn't picking all the beat-driven pop songs, which I was writing to please the label, he was picking the musical ones.

The beat-driven ones were packed off to Brothers in Rhythm and all the other trendy producers we were working with. Chris was choosing all these simple lovely songs and producing them beautifully for me.

When I gave Chris 'Back for Good' he said, 'Jesus Christ,' and immediately started booking all these amazing guitarists to work on it,

Everyone was like, 'Oh, as soon as I heard that song I knew it was going to be a smash . . .' Hmmn. They didn't. Despite Chris's faith in that track, what's weird is no one else really spotted its potential.

The label chose 'Sure' as the first single off that album, which was us trying to be Boyz II Men. Not even Boyz II Men, they were singing proper songs. 'Sure' was an OK song, but let's be honest, derivative and forgettable.

There I was, wearing ridiculous costumes and showing my bare arse in videos and deep down, inspired by Chris, I was wondering, Where's that guy gone that used to just play the piano?

'Back for Good' was me getting him back. 'Back for Good' invited the old me out of the closet. That was the magic of that song. 'Back for Good' is not about a girl, it's about a piano.

I had been writing songs like this for years already when I joined the band, and I was constantly told, 'Oh, you need to pack that in, it doesn't sound like it'll make the charts. Forget that boring piano, lad. Go and press buttons.' The real crux of it is I was being told, 'You don't fit in. Put away who you are, be more bad.'

How many artists do we know who get a record deal and are then immediately told to be different, look different, act different, sound different?

Fortunately the song was successful. Can you imagine if it wasn't and that was my chance blown?

'Back for Good' is only four chords. The one thing that took me ages to learn was that simplicity because I'd come from playing ten chords every second, being a whizz on a keyboard. It was really difficult for me to make simple music. Less is more, as the Modernist architect Corbusier said, something millions of artists of every kind have gone on to agree with.

The best pop music is *very* simple. I had to put away all those twiddly clever skills I learned on the keyboards as a teenager. I didn't pull them out again until I started doing musicals in my forties.

But of course I arrived in the band thinking, Oh right, I just want to show off here, I can do this, this, and this. And look, I can do this too. And it's too much. All the producers we worked with were like, 'It's too many, way too many chords. These melodies all over the place are just too much. Stop trying to impress. Keep it simple, only use so many chords. Chill out!'

So I learned painfully how to simplify what I was doing.

So 'Back for Good' might only have four chords but that doesn't mean you can't go to town with the recording.

A lot of that track was recorded in my house. Not many people had home studios in 1994 because the kit then required a massive room. Wires, lumpy mixing desks, and then there's all the extra power that needed to be brought into the house.

As soon as Chris Porter heard 'Back for Good' he had Phil Palmer on the next plane to Manchester from France. He arrived late afternoon. I'd never 'flown in' a musician before and especially not one known as Eric Clapton's favourite session guitarist. It felt big time. Mum and Dad had come over for dinner. I like to think I cooked spaghetti Bolognese, but I think Mum probably did. After dinner we spent the whole night recording Phil's parts. High parts, low parts, stereo tracking, then retuning the guitar for a 'fuller wash'. I had never seen production like this before. It was meticulous and resulted in this luscious wall of acoustic guitars that underpinned the sound and rhythm for this pop song I'd written. Glen Campbell would have been proud.

The next morning Chris packed the car and we drove to Abbey Road Studios to record the strings. I'd never been there before and was beside myself. I was pretty cocky at that time, things were going very well. But at Abbey Road I was just wow, wow, just, bloody *wow*, as a thirty-two-strong string section played my song. It was the most incredible sound I'd ever heard.

Chris made me stand in the studio on the first run-through so I could hear them play with my actual real-life ears, which is so different to listening through speakers or headphones.

He went off, mixed the song and the rest is history. I think we might just have stayed a cheesy boyband if 'Back for Good' hadn't happened. Once you've written a good song, they can't take that away from you. Even people who make a thing of saying they hate boybands, hate us, hate me, will come over and tell me, 'I love that song.'

Everything that went on that record was sculpted. The piano voicing, the backing vocals – it was all extremely *music*. It was profoundly thrilling for me, and everything I loved about this obsession with music that drove me on and on and on. It was a massive step up for us. And it did well. Number one in 30 countries, including America, and it caught the attention of the great record man Clive Davis in New York. It's by far the most streamed song I've written, about 160 million times as I'm writing this. Weirdly, the band the label wanted us to sound like, Boyz II Men, went on and covered it a few years later. I still think Take That's version is better, we owned that song.

Every time I record strings, you know, I still do that thing. The first time they play I always go and just listen with my own ears. Thank you, Chris Porter.

I think we might just have stayed a cheesy boyband if 'Back for Good' hadn't happened. Once you've written a good song, they can't take that away from you.

# ROBBIE WILLIAMS LEAVES TAKE THAT

*'Lads, I'm leaving the band.'*

The Take That audience always felt like a big gang friendship, we'd grown up together really. Being a teenager can be hard, say your parents split up, or school's a battleground, or you've fallen out of favour with the mean gang. I don't know for sure, but I think the Take That audiences always felt, 'This is my happy place. This is where it's safe.'

The fans were always on our minds and when Rob left I knew they were going to be really upset. Jason was always into telling the truth, telling it how it is, but the rest of us understood that the fans didn't want the unvarnished truth.

Robbie leaving seemed like an enormous event to the outside world. The mid-nineties were different to now, life was fairly simple. Robbie going was news in a way I doubt very much it would be today. Who knows.

Inside our Take That world of us five, yes, he left, he left the room. He took an orange, as I remember it, a melon, according to him. He got in his car with the blacked-out windows and he was driven off.

But we didn't really believe he'd gone.

We thought he'd be back in the morning.

Probably he was just tired like the rest of us.

And we were tired.

It had been six years of people telling us what to do non-stop. There was always a stylist, a vocal coach or a choreographer riding our arses, or a stage director telling us where to stand and what time to show up in the morning, or a photographer asking us to do ludicrous hyper-happy poses. And Nigel, hustling, cajoling, steering, bossing and busting our asses twenty-four/seven.

We'd all had enough. Being told what to do can only go on for so long. There's a sell-by date and ours was well overdue. Even the elephants at the circus in Blackpool got to have a walk on the beach. When was mine coming?

When we realised the following afternoon that Robbie wasn't coming back I felt a bit jealous that I wasn't the one who'd stood up and said, 'Up yours, I wanna have some fun. I'm a pop star, I'm going to behave like one for a bit.'

It was an interesting time. None of us wanted to leave Take That, but watching someone else leave I – we all – couldn't help but think about taking the leap too. What would being on the outside be like? Rob's departure was a change in direction for him and the turning point of his career. And, a little nod to the man, it is also the reason I wear the red Adidas tracksuit top in *A Different Stage*, because that was what Robbie was pictured in at Glastonbury as he started his new adventure.

By the following night we were hearing stories he was on a boat in the South of France with Paula Yates. Again, I felt jealous.

I'm in an army barracks rehearsing dance moves in Stockport and Rob's on the Côte d'Azur with George bloody Michael.

Robbie Williams announced he was leaving the band on 17 July 1995. We were three months into the *Nobody Else* tour and he'd been off getting battered with Britpop stars at Glastonbury Festival and drifting further away from the Take That mothership.

It had run its course. Rob had gone.

Helplines were set up for the fans who were devastated.

Our tight bubble, our inner circle, had been infiltrated. Suddenly everyone had a Robbie story, all of which were more or less the same – 'I saw Rob last night off his face at a party with a hot model.'

I won't pretend it wasn't dispiriting but we put our heads down and got on with it. *Nobody Else* was a big tour, the biggest we'd ever done.

We had a lot of work to do, we always did.

It was the beginning of the end.

# TAKE THAT'S OVER

*'. . . everybody! I'm still here!'*

'Thanks for everybody's support over the last five years, you have been fantastic to us but unfortunately the rumours are true. "How Deep is Your Love" will be our last single together and *Greatest Hits* will be our last album. And from today, there is no more.'

And with those words, it was done.

When I look back and try to pinpoint when the wheels started to come off, it's when we had a few number ones under our belt, when the success sank in. We weren't kids any more, we were young men, and slowly the tide started to turn.

We had a lot less respect for the manager. These kids he'd raised wanted a bit of independence. They didn't want to be told they couldn't have a girlfriend.

And we were tired, we'd worked non-stop for six years. Especially me. We'd worked until we started to resent it.

We kept the band going for a bit after he walked out, but with Rob gone it never felt the same. We announced we were breaking up seven months after Robbie left, on 13 February 1996.

Everyone was in agreement, Take That had run its course. It was absolutely sincere what Mark said, 'We do care an awful lot about the fans and we hope the fans will understand . . .'

The papers reported that my voice was cracking with emotion, but honestly, I wasn't feeling too emotional. In fact I couldn't wait to get on with the Take That business we had left to do – a single, a farewell tour – and crack on with the rest of my brilliant life.

News outlets were describing me as 'the most likely to make a success of life after Take That'. Likely? Actually, if you don't mind! I was certain. In fact, I used the press conference to announce us splitting up to also announce my imminent solo career. One of the music industry's most legendary star makers, Clive Davis, was waiting in New York, New York to sign me to his label, Arista.

# DAWN BARLOW

*I'm not alone.*

I had met Dawn a few times over the years. She was a brilliant professional dancer and she'd worked with us on videos, tours and TV shows. We'd first worked together, in fact, in the eighties, when I very briefly threw off the chains of being a Gary Barlow, and adopted a new stage persona as a singer called Kurtis Rush.

Kurtis didn't work out, but after a few shy sideways glances over the last decade, my God, Dawn and me did. I properly met Dawn on our final tour and here's why I really abandoned Rob. I didn't call him or get in touch because I'd fallen in LOVE, and big time. I was completely Dawn mad.

Mum brought us up. Ask Our Ian, Dad was there, in the background, but it was Marjorie Barlow, our mum, there day in, day out. It's the same in our house. Dawn's always there, always present for the kids. I'm there when I can be, but one of the downsides of what I do is that music and TV suck up huge chunks of time.

She's never thrown it back at me, not once. She manages me, the kids, our home; she has a business, she didn't retire from dancing for ages after we married. She's been the rock in our family, for us, and then there's the beasts, the hamsters and guinea pigs that come and go, our two dogs and the pet elephant in the room, fame. Must be a bloody nightmare. She's written the book on being married to the business; well, she hasn't, she bloody hates attention. But she did write these thirteen things . . .

# THIRTEEN THINGS I'VE LEARNED ABOUT BEING MARRIED TO A POP STAR

## BY DAWN BARLOW

## 01

When he's on tour he's more distracted; he's in a different time zone to the rest of the family. He goes to bed late, gets up late and although he absolutely loves it, he worries endlessly about getting ill because if he does he lets down everyone, including the fans who he is very committed to.

## 02

I've never wished he was an accountant or a bank manager. I used to dance and we met several times working before we got together. It's always felt totally natural for me to end up with a performer.

## 03

When he's writing songs he's very insular and focused. There are different stages to the process but I suppose the part that drives us all mad is when you think he's listening to you and you ask a question and he will snap out of his daydream and just say, 'Which one?' It's his go-to answer to every single question and when he says it I know he hasn't heard a word anyone's said.

## 04

He will never switch off, not really. On holiday he won't be able to stop working. He will always sneak off to catch up on emails. And even if he didn't, holidays give him the space to think and that's when songs, ideas or lyrics pop into his head.

## 05

He's pretty handy round the house when he's home. He's always happy to pop to the shop for milk. If they can't go to the corner shop for milk then you're living in the wrong neighbourhood, or with the wrong pop star.

## 06

Red carpets are horrendous – you'd think I'd be used to it when the photographers ask for Gary on his own, waving you to one side like a bad smell. I've never got used to standing to one side and looking like a lemon. My tactic now is to run up the carpet first, then he can slowly make his way up, showing all his best sides to the camera. That's more comfortable for both of us.

## 07

The thought of being famous makes me feel very uncomfortable. I can't get past that. That may be why our marriage is rock solid. He's more than welcome to all the limelight.

## 08

Sometimes we find ourselves in a place where no one knows who he is. That place will immediately become my favourite place in the world.

## 09

I find it very hard when people approach us when we are trying to spend time together as a couple or with the kids. The worst is at dinner, there's a certain type of person who will come over after staring at you for ages and the opening line is always, 'Sorry for bothering you . . . ' – well, they're obviously not that sorry otherwise they'd not do it – 'but can we have a photo?'

## 10

I can tell straight away if someone's starstruck as they usually have a rash on their neck, especially the women.

## 11

Being a musician and an entertainer is written in his genes. He just absolutely loves his job. He can't not do it. There's never going to be a time when he retires and plays golf.

## 12

The key to staying married to someone like Gary is to have a little patience. Have a lot of patience, actually.

## 13

If I could give one piece of advice to someone just starting a relationship with an artist, then it would be: Don't fight it.

# CLIVE DAVIS

*'You've had a call . . . from America.'*

Davis is a titan among twentieth-century music executives. In 1973 he created Arista Records, and in 1997 he signed me. A few other things happened in between, like, he created or honed the careers of Whitney Houston, Billy Joel, Pink Floyd, Alicia Keys, Bruce Springsteen, Aretha Franklin, Miles Davis, Bob Dylan, Janis Joplin and Simon and Garfunkel. *Simon and Garfunkel.*

For a Frodsham boy, even one who has grown so accustomed to hit records and success, this is the biggest deal of my life.

There's a name for Clive's ilk in the business, they're what's known as 'a great record man'.

A great record man will be ferocious at the business, ruthless as hell, on top of contract law, accounting and the machinery of running big and often multiple companies.

It looks attractive, doesn't it, to be a pop star? But when you realise as an artist that you are the assets, the human stocks and shares the executives trade in, the sheen comes off.

So a great record man could navigate the murky waters of the business like a great white shark but he will also have what's known as 'ears'. Having 'ears' means you can spot an artist with the potential to perform like a blue chip stock, i.e. hit after hit, smash after smash, great touring stamina. Clive wasn't just known for his ears, they were said to be platinum. Clive's a legend.

The names of the great record men are huge in the business. Ahmet Ertegun, who signed the Stones and countless amazing others. Berry Gordy, who founded Motown. Walter Yetnikoff didn't have Clive's 'ears' but he was famous for forcing MTV to play Michael Jackson videos when the channel only played white rock.

These guys are usually lawyers by trade but in the early days they would often have been gangsters and fraudsters. There's an incredible book about them all called *Hit Men*, by Fredric Dannen. It's a shocker!

Clive Davis is a smart guy and very hard working. The son of an electrician from Brooklyn, he was orphaned at 17 but still won a scholarship to Harvard Law School at a time when sons of electricians from Brooklyn weren't too common there. He's a New Yorker, born and bred, with characteristic smarts and the hustle in equal doses.

Clive had recently graduated from Harvard when he started working as a lawyer for Columbia Records. Five years later he was running the company. He went on to start Arista Records, and two crucial Black-run labels for hip hop, 'urban' and R&B: Bad Boy Records with Sean 'Puffy' Combs and LaFace Records with LA Reid and Babyface.

And now the great record man, the one with the platinum ears, wants me.

# CONCORDE

*Sitting on Concorde, listening to my new single.*

I'm usually quite careful not to sound an entitled dickhead, but I'm gonna risk it here. I do feel sorry for the artists of today that they'll never fly on Concorde.

I loved Concorde.

In the time I was signed to Clive Davis' label, which, we will soon discover, wasn't very long, I must have flown the London–New York route on Concorde thirty times.

Up there, that high, the sky is dark blue, it's almost space. The atmosphere was so different the plane grew six inches in the air. Travelling at nearly 1,400mph, twice the speed of sound, means everyone beneath you gets a hell of a sonic boom as you fly overhead. Meanwhile, you're up in the sky being offered caviar and Krug.

Inside the tiny cabin, the seats were tiny, the windows tiny and the noise, the noise was massive and part of the thrill. It was impossible not to get a little smile as it took off. And then, as a frequent Concorde flyer, I would look at the earth curving below me, throw my big coat over my head and go to sleep. Three hours later, I was there!

The pilot would always warn us that taking off was going to be pretty full on. And it was, it was like taking off in a spaceship.

Meanwhile, Einstein here has calculated that you could leave London at breakfast and be in New York five hours behind for another breakfast before you ate the first one. Mad! I liked to fly on the 10am flight out of New York because it meant despite a five-hour time difference I got home in time to go out for dinner.

Once, I used my credit card to buy Dawn some perfume at JFK and then that night I took her out for Japanese. I went to pay and, 'Sir, there is a problem with your card.' It was not humanly possible I was buying perfume for my girlfriend at ten in New York and could be back eating sashimi with her at six in Kensington. It must be fraud.

Nope. It must be Concorde.

# 'LOVE WON'T WAIT': THE POWER AND PERILS OF THE REMIX

*I turned and honestly walked off the stage to the sound of my own feet.*

'Love Won't Wait' was originally written in 1994 for Madonna by Madonna with Shep Pettibone, the producer who created 'Vogue' with her.

This song lands on Clive's desk and he sends it to me. The song sounds odd. But they're all convinced. Clive and I have just started working together. He's found the song, and Jesus, it's by *Madonna*. I'm . . . I'm . . . well, I'm semi-convinced.

I find Steve Lipson who's worked with Annie Lennox a lot. He worked with so many eighties greats creating beautiful, classy pop music – Simple Minds, Grace Jones, Lionel Richie. We both get to work and by the end of the week have a song to send to Clive. He says, 'It's fantastic. What are you doing tomorrow night? This is so good I want you to come and sing at the Grammy party.'

He asks me to fly over on Concorde the next day to launch me at his party that night. The other artist he's launching is Sean Combs, Puffy.

This is it. Clive's party at the Plaza, the place where people leap off the stage and into the big time. This is a big-time opportunity.

Clive sends the tune to be remixed by Junior Vasquez, this don of the underground dance music scene in New York.

Remix is a word associated with dance music but it's just as normal to remix something in a pop style. 'Never Forget' was a remix by Jim Steinman. The remix can be more famous than the original song, like Toni Braxton's 'Un-Break My Heart', or John Legend's 'All of Me'.

I love a remix, I've had loads of success with them over the years. People don't realise 'Pray' is a remix. The original is a very simple ballad but Steve Jervier remixed it with a sample from Soul II Soul's 'Back to Life', which gave 'Pray' wings to get to number one and stay there for a month in the summer of '93.

Nowt wrong with a remix, baby! 'Could It Be Magic', our cover version of the Barry Manilow song, was turned into a killer dance floor track by the Rapino Brothers, who were famous for their Italian House music.

A remix means someone takes the original song and changes the music. It can be very subtle, or it can be like the one Clive played me when I arrived at the party venue with a couple of hours before the show started on 12 February 1997.

He'd taken everything identifiable from the rhythm, the melody, the structure.

For about ninety seconds it was just these tribal, war-like drums. The music had been replaced by these clanky, bone-rattling samples. I tell you what it sounded like – the lifts that bring the miners out of the pit. Then half of the first chorus before it goes back to the verse, except the verse is the chorus. You get the picture . . .

Brilliant if you're off your face at Twilo at 5am, I can only imagine.

As soon as I hear it I think, There's no way I'm doing that. What I get wrong is I don't say it out loud. I know it's wrong for me. But I'm a kid from Frodsham. And Clive is a hit man. He is never wrong, I'll perform to this remix at the Grammy party.

What do I say? 'I don't think we should do that, Clive . . .'

What happens next is burned on my memory. This is my whole life's dream, and it's turning into a nightmare.

I try to get across my misgivings about the remix but no one's listening, everyone's already up and marching me to the rehearsal. 'Clive, you know this, this version. I don't, I don't think we should do this tonight.'

We get to the stage and he boots an act off. 'Gary's on now.'

As I'm singing he's waving left, waving right, showing me how he wants me to move round the stage – 'Centre, centre, right . . .' – while also shouting out instructions on how to sing to this massive, clanking, 5am-in-a-nightclub remix. All I'm thinking is, I need to learn this, I cannot do this tonight. 'Clive, I don't think we can do this.'

I told the A&R, 'We shouldn't be doing this tonight. We really . . .'

An assistant grabs me, 'Gary, quick, this way. We're going to do some interviews.'

We go through these double doors and outside there are all these people queuing for the legendary Clive Davis pre-Grammy party. I walk into a wall of press interviews, CNN, MTV. All these people are saying, 'Hey, we heard that single, "Back for Good", love it, love it.'

I'm going on in an hour and I still don't know the song. 'Hey, listen guys, when are we gonna rehearse the song?'

The more the fear builds in me, the less people seem to hear my voice. 'Hey, Gary, we've got your suit . . .'

'I need to rehearse, I need to talk to Clive. NO MORE INTERVIEWS!'

Clive appears. 'Gary, there's a full house!'

I spend the last ten minutes trying to learn the song while people are dressing me, fussing over me, doing my hair, make-up. It feels like I'm on death row. And then I hear the words, 'He's come all the way from London, England . . .'

My heart's pounding, my mouth's dry. All I've had all day is people, people, people, fussing and pushing me from one thing to another. Four people push me onto the stage and the music starts right away and it's so loud that I've lost count of the beat. I cannot hear where I'm due to come in and start singing. I missed the first chorus going on and now I'm starting to forget the words to my own song because I'm thinking, Clive said I need to dance here, move over there.

I look out and see Bobby Brown with his back to the stage.

It's the longest ten minutes of my life. It's a disaster.

I walk off that stage to the sound of my own footsteps and people talking amongst themselves. There is no applause.

All day I've been fussed over and surrounded by people. You know the worst thing of all? I come off stage and there's nobody. It's like I'm radioactive.

Meanwhile, Puff Daddy is on stage and people are going crazy.

I walk out of the theatre and out the front of the Rockefeller Plaza. It's empty. It's pouring with rain and I just walk ten blocks to the Royalton Hotel where I'm staying.

The problem with Clive was simple. He never liked my music. He liked 'Back for Good'. And that was it. He was always trying to push me in a direction that I wasn't suited for. Very soon you lose touch with who you are and what your musical identity is. It all becomes a jumble of you, them and what's currently doing well in the charts.

I think the Grammy party symbolised too much for me. It was like that small injury that ends up throwing your whole body out of whack. Performing to remixes is part of the job, things do sometimes go wrong, but the 'Love Won't Wait' remix broke something.

There will be someone like Clive Davis at every label – a kingmaker who discovers the biggest-selling talent. But that doesn't mean he's never wrong. For every Whitney, I reckon there's forty more like me.

The moral of this story is, if you've got a voice, no matter who you are, and you feel something is wrong, you've got to pipe up. I go back to this memory again and again, like a dog returns to its vomit. It was an incredibly tough way to learn a lesson. The fact is, I'd have been better off saying, 'I'm going home.'

# THEME FROM NEW YORK, NEW YORK
*The sound of the end of a career.*

Feels like it's existed for Frank Sinatra since his huge chapter in the Great American Songbook first opened. But actually, 'New York, New York' was written for his goddaughter, Liza Minnelli. It was the title track of the 1977 film *New York, New York*, directed by Martin Scorsese.

It was written by the genius songwriting duo of Fred Ebb and John Kander, who wrote *Cabaret* and *Chicago*. Liza's version in the Scorsese film is very cabaret, very theatrical, full of drama, passion, energy, yet always there's that professional control. It's very good, the lady owns it.

Which is cool, but not quite as cool as seeing Liza singing it live at the Statue of Liberty's hundredth anniversary at Meadowlands in 1986. Only an American can deliver a tune like that. It's a whole emotional life right there for you in a three-minute song. The way she holds that last note. Million-dollar money note!

However, this tune found global fame when Frank Sinatra covered it a year or so later. Sinatra hated 'My Way' in the last decades of his life, whereas his biographer told the *New York Times* that Sinatra described 'New York, New York' as 'one of the most exciting pieces of music of all of my years'.

This was all happening in the late seventies when New York was a famously dangerous city, albeit to a soundtrack of disco. Sinatra's version of 'New York, New York' became a rallying cry, a proud celebratory song.

And like so many songs, it happened fast and by accident almost, because Robert de Niro had rejected the original theme song for the Scorsese film. John Kander told the *New York Times* recently that he and Ebb had 'dashed off' 'New York, New York' in forty-five minutes to placate de Niro.

If you can make it there you can make it ANYWHERE! This tune fills the room with skyscrapers, ambition, dreams, yellow cabs, neon lights, Broadway . . . and, in the case of my life at this particular point, with my hopes of cracking America fading fast, the crashing reality that my own dreams are trickling through my fingers like sand.

Once that mean, self-critical voice in your head has been given a stage, it's there to stay.

# HUBRIS

*Except it got worse . . .*

In the dictionary it says, 'excessive pride or confidence', but hubris is more than that. It's the pride that comes before a fall.

You don't need to have studied Classics at Cambridge University to know the story of Icarus, who wanted to fly and made wings from feathers and wax, but flew too high and near to the sun with his wings made of wax and . . . Icarus forgot that we're not invincible. We're only people.

Hubris is one of Tim's words. 'Hubris, Gary, is when you're peas above sticks as they say in Manchester, when you're too big for your boots and stop being able to walk any further. Then you fall over!'

It's from Ancient Greece. In their plays, poems and stories the audience would be sitting judging the main character as they behaved in a way that was certain to lead to their downfall. Their Nemesis, as they called it, was the person, event or heavenly intervention that helped that downfall along, that stuck a foot out as they clattered forward in their hubris boots.

Was this me? Was Robbie my Nemesis? Or maybe Clive? I don't know.

Up until this point, it felt like everything I did was just magnificent. When I arrived in New York for the Grammy party, I had the biggest wingspan. I flew so high I looked down on the earth from a seat on Concorde – a lot higher than Icarus, I can tell you.

When I crept back on to Concorde for the return journey after the party, I'd had them wings clipped.

Now at this point in a Greek tragedy, the fella limps off having learned a lesson and that's the end of that. And to an extent, this is true. That slow humiliation humbled me permanently. I'd never get the glorious, furious, focused self-belief of my teens and twenties back. I'd like to say that this was a good thing. That I needed it. That it made me the man I am today. That I learned a lesson . . .

Nope. Not playing.

It was an incredible feeling inside that amazing golden world of supreme confidence and self-belief all the time. From 'Back for Good' until Clive Davis' Grammy party, I was carried on everyone's shoulders. I was writing great song after great song. The air permanently glistened.

And why be an arsehole to someone when you're on top of the world? What is the point? That's not how my mum and dad brought me up.

When we were in the band, I was always the one saying, 'We've got to keep our feet on the ground.' Rob wanted to go off and do red-carpet parties and hang out with cool people.

My self-belief was just insane, but what I wanted to do more than anything was work, to grow creatively and make music. Out of all of us I had the greatest self-belief. I deserved to be here, and I wanted to go higher, further, the band was never enough. There would be my solo career. There would be my own record company, it'd have a hundred employees, I'd create an alternative to the frustrating music industry. I was going to change the world.

And maybe I could have done.

When you have self-belief you are the funniest guy in the room. I was at an event once with loads of other artists and Bono got up to talk: 'Having a hit record, isn't it great. You're taller, fitter, a better husband, funnier . . .'

But once self-belief is gone, everything shifts. The Grammy party was a broken cog in the whole machinery of me. Deep down, I knew it was over that night. Clive and I limped on for another year or so until I was dropped by the label in the US, and then here in the UK.

Once that mean, self-critical voice in your head has been given a stage, it's there to stay. Mine might not always be shouting quite as loud as it did in that period when I lost my deal and started wearing bigger and bigger cardigans, but once it's got its crucial audience of one, up there on its stage right by your ear, you can't get the bugger off your shoulder.

# ACT II

# ACT II

## THE MILLENNIUM

*For the first time in my life, music wasn't making things better.*

If you're expecting an exciting revisit to the end of the twentieth century and the start of the third millennium, you'll find no fireworks here at Delamere Manor.

As the clock tipped from 1999 to 2000 I was quietly, steadily over-eating in the tiny TV room with the massive telly in my house with so many rooms I never managed to count them all, overlooking a six-acre lake on my 117-acre country estate. A pop-star mansion I didn't feel at home in.

Apparently, it took four hours for my ex-bandmate and his writing partner to create the song not just of the century but of the 'Millennium' – as he cannily called his 1998 number one single. Not quite as impressive as Kander and Ebb's forty-five minutes for 'New York, New York', but more painful to listen to.

It would be given an exhaustingly massive amount of airtime between its release in 1998, just as I was getting acquainted with hubris, and now, here in the year 2000, stuffed with beige food, Quality Street and Southern Comfort and lemonade. Two chords of torture in D Flat major.

Meanwhile, to me, the man who wrote 'Back for Good' as a love song to his piano, the keys looked like the jaws of a crocodile.

Slowly expanding into bigger and bigger cardigans of despair, I was too scared to go out of the gates. Eating my feelings. As the tabloid newspapers liked to note every time they published a photo of me, I was fat.

I think only boybands back then had a clue about the kind of scrutiny women were expected to cope with their whole lives. I had a six-pack for most of the Take That years, I was a normal-sized kid when Nigel took me on. Yet Simon Cowell likes to joke that he turned down signing Take That to Sony in the early days with the words, 'Fire the fat one and I'll sign the band.'

People spoke like that then, it was OK to fat bash.

My confidence was shot, I had become terrified of my piano, I went to my studio most days only to pretend to work.

Weed, fags, coffee, booze and beige food were a way to take the pain away. All these fixes, like a pint of Jack Daniels and Coke in the evening to get you to sleep, were brilliant. Brilliant only in the short term. Then they made you feel worse. What's gonna fix it? More of the same.

I took eight sugars and that weird powdered cream in my instant coffee, I ate sugar all day until I stopped eating and started drinking it, I smoked like the chimneys at Ellesmere Port Chemical Plant.

I was someone without a use trying to find something to do with their hands. I'd go the extra distance to the petrol station where they never recognised me and buy my preferred combination of Silk Cut Ultra Low (healthy fags) and Marlboro Lights (full-fat smokes).

I liked them a little bit stale, so they crackled and I could hear them. I chain-smoked, one after the other, listening to the crackle. Music, of sorts.

I wrote a bit at the studio with my old friend Eliot Kennedy. Then El would leave. My heart wasn't in it.

And I ate.

I'd always liked food, chased carbs, sweets. But you know what, I don't blame the pick 'n' mix. Once a week, I used to spend ten pence on sugar. Now there was a steady drip of something sweet or stodgy going into my body, my blood sugar levels were permanently elevated. I wasn't exercising, so where could my body put that sugar? It was all safely tucked away under a selection of zip-up Dad cardigans.

I didn't even listen to music then – quite an extreme situation for someone who's made music their whole life. Where music was then, in the charts, was more about snarling and sarcasm. Take That wouldn't have had a place in the British music scene as it was then. All Blur and Oasis taking pot shots at each other. Everyone banging on endlessly about who they hated. 'Never Forget' was our seventh number one, a euphoric song about the ups and downs of life. It was knocked off by Blur's 'Country House', with lyrics that take the piss out of the band's manager and his new 'very big house in the country', with a video directed by the artist Damien Hirst.

It was everything I wasn't. Our media, our country, our British way – we love it when it's all mean, dark and edgy. Maybe it's those long grey days, and the wind.

Our Ian would have loved being a part of all that, he would have loved going toe to toe with Liam Gallagher at the Brit Awards. And Rob. He fitted that mould so well, he played it well, he had come from a broken home, he had his struggles. But there was no place for Gary Barlow from Frodsham inside Cool Britannia.

Robbie was the kid with plastic wheels. My BMX had metal spokes.

That guy on Concorde? He was long gone.

The thing is, Take That had success on enormous stages. The fire that lights inside you, the experience of it, it's huge. The fire feels like it's gone out.

I think I was depressed, I don't know for sure. Right or wrong, my upbringing made me challenge this. My mum's a stoic woman. Her dad died when she was 11. She cared for the family as her own mum struggled with the grief of losing her husband. She has never, ever complained about this or talked about how tough it was. And it must have been tough. You see, the Barlow way is to keep going. That's what I saw growing up.

I kept saying to myself, 'It'll be all right. Keep going.'

One foot in front of the other.

# KIDS

*. . . surrounded by young people wanting me to come up with music they could dance to.*

The cardigan years were by no means all bad. We'd just had kids. And they are amazing. Dan in 2000, Emily eighteen months later. They turn your life upside down – but try not to complain because before you know it, it's over.

So I did, if I am honest, play the piano from time to time. I put my fingers in the crocodile's jaws to play 'The Wheels on the Bus' on the grand piano in the lounge. The minute my fingers hit the keys the children started running round and round the piano. They loved it. It was a way to wear them out because Dan, our oldest, wasn't doing much sleeping.

It felt like he didn't sleep for four years until he could get out and run and fight other kids. The only music we ever found that could make him sit still for longer than thirty seconds was Baby Mozart. The music came out of a toy you wound up and we'd watch him listen in a happy stupor as he had his 'so-called' bedtime milk (so-called because it was never bedtime for Dan), like a man supping his last pint in the pub.

But we didn't mind, he's our first child. Despite the fact he never slept, it was just lovely. Once you've got a second, things change. One's magic. Two's work. You might as well have six. When I meet people with three kids under five, I give them a sympathetic look. That's brutal.

Emily arrived and Dan got even louder. Our first daughter has always been good as gold, I think she knew there was no room for two toddler tyrants in our house.

Having said that, you do get better at it, and by the time we had Daisy we were pros. Baby Daisy had the best of us.

The world revolves around our kids. That's normal. But I wanted to go to work, I grew up in a house where you get up and go and do a day's work.

I didn't have any work. I felt useless. I'd be looking out the window at my studio. I couldn't see a future, and that's the worst. My career was over, it was gone. I was thinking, How am I going to support my family for the next fifty years until I die?

When they went to school and the other kids asked, 'What does your daddy do?' my kids would say, 'He sits at home staring at a piano.'

# 'THE WHEELS ON THE BUS'

*'The wheels on the bus go round and round . . . round and round . . .'*

'The Wheels on the Bus' was written by an American folk musician called Verna Hills in 1939. It was, apparently, an instant hit with kids and has remained so to this day. Why?

Children's music is not much different to pop music. As a pop songwriter you have to learn, always, to keep it simple. Pop has the same hypnotic, rhythmical, memorable quality as a nursery rhyme, but with a splash of adult sophistication.

As adults, when we hear a hook, the bit you remember, we aren't that different to our child selves asking our parents to sing a song to us, again, and again, and again. And again, Daddy.

'The wheels on the bus go round and round, round and round, round and round . . .'

A good pop song is very simple. It has energy, it's happy, up, exciting. People both remember it *and dance* to it. To get up and dance is a liberating thing, but it gets harder the older and more inhibited and buttoned-up we become as adults. If your music gets the listener's body moving so their inner child can play, then you're on to a winner.

And if you can make 'em whistle as well? Put it this way, if your painter and decorator is whistling your song, that's affirmation way bigger than any award.

A big concert in the Queen's garden called Party at the Palace? Pathetic rubbish.

That's just rubbish!

THE QUEEN'S GOLDEN JUBILEE 2002

# JUBILEE '02

*The fear of anyone ever finding out.*

I loved being a dad but inside something was broken. The last Jubilee was in 1977, when a younger me clocked that music made things better. This Jubilee, the Queen's fiftieth year on the throne, things could not have been more different.

Round this time, the cardigan years, I couldn't really write music. I worked a bit in tandem with my brilliant friend Eliot Kennedy. I don't know if El realised, but he was carrying me.

I'm low.

Minds are mysterious. I am constantly amazed by the way my mind gives me music, lyrics, ideas, sometimes without even being conscious of it. It's an extraordinary thing, the human mind. Some people say it is as mysterious as the universe.

The man who introduced the world to psychology over one hundred years ago, Sigmund Freud, said, 'Unexpressed emotions never die. They are buried alive and will come forth later in uglier ways.'

Is this why I was bulimic at this time? I purged in darkness, in private, alone, in the farthest corners of my pop-star mansion. I was ashamed of my bulimia. Was that my shame at what had happened with my career and all the feelings I had that I couldn't make sense of? Was the bulimia my 'unexpressed emotions . . . come forth in uglier ways'?

Outside I was still upbeat and apparently quite confident. I was pretending – of course. It wasn't the real me though, because who I was at that time was what I call the King Rubbisher. I was cynical.

In that period, everything was rubbish. When the Queen celebrated her Golden Jubilee in 2002, instead of celebrating all the music and the parties, I'd say, 'Ugh, what's this Jubilee rubbish? Brian May on the roof of Buckingham Palace playing "God Save the Queen" on his Red Special guitar he built from scratch. That's not the British answer to Jimi Hendrix playing "The Star-Spangled Banner". That's just rubbish! A big concert in the Queen's garden called Party at the Palace? Pathetic rubbish.'

But there was still a bit of the old Gary left – an inner me thought it was pretty cool. The good man was still there. He was struggling to get out of the miserable cardigan. He was thinking that an all-star band made up of not just pop stars but theatre stars too, all up on stage together in the gardens of the palace, was pretty lovely.

Inner me knew that was good, and that means the old Gary was still in there.

And no bloody Robbie either. Phew!

# FILA TRAINERS

*I used to throw some shapes in these . . .*

Trainers were massive back in the late eighties and early nineties. They still are, you might say, but by massive I don't mean popular, I mean really bloody big. As in, they took up a lot of space. My red Filas cost £24.99 in 1989. They were my dancing shoes in Blackpool, though you'd easily mistake them for the Isle of Wight hovercraft. I'd slip them on at the end of my Talk of the Coast show to signal that we were about to get funky when I started in on Kool & the Gang.

The Filas weren't great for dancing in because, actually, they were bloody awful for dancing in. They were heavy, wide, cumbersome, and could possibly have been quite dangerous for running. But they looked great. And that's what mattered.

Fila was a big brand in the late eighties and early nineties. All the rave kids and club kids wore them, but not to the gym. Up north, street wear was all about big trainers and a big coat.

Get ready, Blackpool, the red Filas are on. These were fancy tackle.

They were part of our Take That look too, we all had them. All the original Thatters remember us wearing them on *The Hitman and Her*, which was this late-night TV show that toured the nightclubs, sort of *Top of the Pops* with repetitive beats. Like our devil horns, the Filas ended up part of our earliest stage looks.

When I joined the band, Jason had a pair exactly the same, and he'd been a dancer on *The Hitman and Her*. Jason was dead cool. He didn't even live with his mum any more.

Then Howard got a pair.

Now mine looked a bit battered next to them from all that running man at Talk of the Coast. So we thought, Fuck it, let's all get a box-fresh pair and make it look nice and symmetrical.

The red Filas are famous with our audience, along with our leather bomber jackets by British Knights – which was not British at all, it was a New-York-based sportswear and trainer label which was popular with hip hop artists. We wore them loads on our first tour in '92. When you see those early shoots with magazines like *Smash Hits*, *Look In*, *My Guy* and *Jackie*, that was our costume.

I would have bought them the first time round for Blackpool because they looked like they were in a show, and we as a band bought them because it was what an organised, professional, proper band does. We put together a strong look to wear on stage.

But these red Filas had been put away at the back of a cupboard, and I only found them rummaging about for something to wear for a run. My first run in a very long time.

I pulled out my old stage shoes and they were like relics from a past life. I'd tucked them away in a dark corner, along with who I was and the dreams I had of who I could be. These Filas have a show graph of their own.

Finding them put me back on the road, literally. They got me running again, and when I swapped the endorphin high of exercise with the miserable short-lived comfort of beige food, everything started to realign. I remember feeling shocked by how incredible I felt after that first run.

The Filas were my Cinderella slippers. I looked at their worn-out soles and remembered all the moves me and the lads had up on that stage. Those memories stirred the embers, they were the spark that would (sorry, got to do this) relight my fire.

# LAS VEGAS, CIRQUE DU SOLEIL AND A SHOW CALLED O
*I thought, God I miss this.*

*O* is a permanent show at the Bellagio Hotel on the main drag in Las Vegas, which is the world's great showtown these days (sorry, Blackpool). It could be called Earth, Wind, Fire and Water because the acrobats perform in all the elements – half of them are former high-level athletes. In *O* they dive in and out of a 1.5-million-gallon swimming pool set up in the hotel with a lake and performing fountains out front in the middle of the Mojave Desert. As you do. Hello, Vegas!

I found myself sitting in the audience on a trip to America with my old friend and collaborator Eliot, 'El'.

We'd been working with Donny Osmond in Utah, a man who radiates American positivity and good vibes. El and I have a rapport and a shared humour that is magic.

We found ourselves with a couple of days to spare. I was feeling good, no one knew me in America (thanks to Clive), I was safe to go to a theatre for the first time in nearly fifteen years – there were no wisecracks about Robbie, no one even looked at me. And by Vegas standards, I was on the slim side. It was all pretty relaxing. My guard was down. It was a beautiful time.

They were queuing round the block for this ticket. It was a hot one. Within seconds of the curtain going up I knew why. Wow! *O* is the work of someone with some serious knowledge of a show graph.

Cirque du Soleil shows are some of the most extraordinary you'll ever see. And they're big, astonishingly ambitious, real spectaculars that cost as much as a massive Hollywood movie to produce. Their shows are all human – no lions, no tigers, no elephants. Just humans doing amazing, jaw-dropping things, set with split-second timing to music from a live symphony orchestra.

But that wasn't what engrossed me. I was watching the audience. Remember, back in the clubs, in Blackpool, while I was up on stage I was constantly watching the audience. All the 'ooohs and aaahs'. I was watching the cogs now, the workings of the show, then I was turning back, looking down my row, watching the audience's reactions.

It lit a spark in me. From the clubs to the Filas to *O*'s insane fiery finale, it's all that same thing. It's all about my love of a show.

I wanted desperately to be on stage again.

Eliot Kennedy and I have a rapport and a shared humour that is magic.

# TAKE THAT ANONYMOUS

*I felt like, for the first time, I was in a band.*

Howard calls. He wants to meet up. There's been an offer.

One of the most interesting nights of my life begins in a bar in a hotel in Kensington in 2005. It's a town-house hotel. Hyde Park is a one-minute walk up the road, the big London museums five minutes down. The bar is dark and comfortable, full of faceless residents, and Mark, Howard and I are just three nobodies. No one's looking.

Mark has a letter in his pocket from Simon Moran, who is a big-deal concert promoter. He's got wind of the fact that our record label, RCA, plans to put out a new Take That greatest hits anthology. (This is standard stuff, they want to try and capitalise on the fact it's been ten years since we split up.) A 'where are they now?' documentary is being made for ITV by Back2Back productions, ostensibly to promote it.

We've had very little to do with all this. But cautiously we've agreed to be involved with the documentary. By now, Robbie is a big deal. A very big star. He's said he 'might'.

Mark gets the letter out. He says he's read it several times and thinks we need to take it seriously. In the old days, Mark was the baby along with Robbie, those two were always clowning around, leaping about. He's got a look on his face I've never seen before.

Serious, determined.

Howard reads it. He's a joker, always making people laugh. A very funny man in all circumstances. (The funniest people come from the north of England – that's a scientifically proven fact.)

I look at Howard, he looks serious. He pushes his bottom teeth forward which indicates he is 'thinking'. I look at Mark.

I read the letter. I can't see it working but I don't want to snuff out the flickering flame of excitement I can see in both their eyes.

There is only one person missing from our Take That Anonymous meeting. We need to ring Jason. Jay was always the grown-up in the band, when we first got together he was the only one who wasn't still living at home with Mummy.

Incredibly, Jay picks up after one ring. Jay never picks up the phone – he's just not that instant guy.

He happens to be south of the river, Wandsworth, he can be there in thirty minutes.

Fuck me. Jay's coming.

The bar manager moves us to a table at the back so we can have more room.

Jay walks in. Opens his arms wide and says, across the room, 'Where's me boys?' And he swaggers across the room like a comedy Manc.

This feels good, this feels like the gang is back together.

Then the banter stops and we start talking. One by one we all download where we've got to in our lives. It's the first time I've admitted to anyone how unhappy I've been. I know Dawn knows, I know Mum and Dad are worried, but I've never discussed it.

Mark, Jay and Howard, they know. Only they could possibly know.

First time round I always wanted to be the leader, I assumed that role. This time round, I don't want to be that guy.

We left each other in 1996 as boys, but that night four adult men sat down to talk. I never wanted to leave, it felt so good to be in their company.

At first only Mark and Howard are into this concert idea. Jay and me aren't so sure. But the four of us have connected and as we talk on, the lads bring us round.

By midnight I'm thinking, 'Bloody hellfires! We need to grab this.' Simon hasn't told anyone else about this proposal. It's just us, we own the space. It's our decision to make. And we're going to say yes.

That night we talked and planned and threw around ideas. The bar kicked us out around three and we went back to my place and carried on talking about tour ideas 'til the sun came up. I told the lads we needed to go to Vegas, to see this show called *O*. I've been back to see that show maybe ten times, with the band, with our set designer and show directors, Es Devlin and Kim Gavin. Every time I work with someone new, I take them to Vegas. I take them to showtown. I take them to Cirque. It's just brilliant.

We had to do it, we had to do this tour.

# THE DOCUMENTARY AND ULTIMATE TOUR

*Stadiums? Bloody hell – we didn't play stadiums the first time round.*

*Take That: For the Record* aired April 2006 on ITV. In seventy minutes it went over the whole nineties story: the gay scene in Manchester, touring the schools and under-18 discos. There's 'Do What U Like', *Top of the Pops*, then the screaming girls, the security nightmares, the sell-out tours, the string of number ones, all the peak boyband madness leading up to Rob leaving and the split that followed in 1996.

Of course what made the documentary really delicious wasn't the success, it was where we all went afterwards in our noughties wilderness, my cardigan years. A place we four were still languishing in. We all had work, sort of, but let's call it what it was.

It was the doldrums for all but one of us five.

Rob the big star gave an interview but never turned up for the big meet-up that was meant to be the climax moment. That was the jeopardy telly needed right there. The scene with us waiting for him made me cringe.

Six million households tuned in and a wave of nostalgia swept through the media and the office water coolers. 'Did you see the Take That documentary?'

The next day our tour was announced and sold out in hours. Only this Simon bloke didn't seem surprised as he booked more dates for us to play stadiums. The only thing bigger than a stadium is, I don't know, the Olympics or something.

We sold nearly half a million tickets in the end.

I couldn't resist the announcement I made at the press conference: 'Thanks for giving us the last ten years off, but unfortunately the rumours are true. Take That are going back on tour.'

# 'PATIENCE'

*Out of all this gratitude for ten years of waiting – a song got born.*

'Patience' is a sea change on so many different levels. We knew very quickly we had to get new music out. We couldn't turn into a nostalgia act and rehash 'Relight' until we could draw our pensions. No one wanted that.

Firstly, when we wrote in the nineties, it was never about our lives. Our lives were just airports and hotels. 'Patience' was the first time Take That's music became more diarised.

'Patience' was the battle cry of a man locked in a cage for a decade. 'Patience' saw me turn into a songwriter who is aware of what's going on inside, a man who doesn't bury his emotions but expresses them. What 'Patience' does is tell the truth.

And 'Patience' was the first time we really wrote together. I never asked the boys to write with me before, I'd wanted it to be all mine. But then hubris stepped in and taught me how valuable these lads were to me and to the music we make.

Take That was made up of men now, all four of us would write. The result was the single 'Patience', which we played to the label knowing they would give us the space to make an album without constant interference.

Both did really well. The single spent a month at number one and a year in the charts. The album, *Beautiful World*, was number one for eight weeks, and between Christmas 2006 and early 2011 it spent 132 weeks in the charts. (Obviously, I don't walk around with all this data in my head, I got it off the official charts website just now as I'm writing.)

All I'm trying to say is, it was clear that people were happy to have us back, and that felt incredible.

# 'RULE THE WORLD'

*. . . the stars are coming out tonight.*

We've flown into Madrid for a radio event, a gig in front of a small audience – maybe 500. We're all – Mark, Jay, Howard and me – waiting in our dressing room before heading on stage. David Beckham has come by – he's still playing for Real Madrid in 2006. All the lads are fussing around him. Everyone loves a visit from David. He's there, he never disappoints, in this amazing leather jacket and a big scarf.

I have this idea, I hear it in my mind's ear, the whole melody and chorus. I lean over to one side and quietly sing it into my phone. Those ideas can go unused for decades sometimes, but I never let an idea pass.

George Michael once said that if he couldn't remember an idea the next day it was no good. I'm not like that. I've got to put it down right then. I get ideas everywhere, and I write them down or make a voice note on my phone.

We go on, sing for an hour, lovely gig, and we fly home. On the way back to London from Madrid, I play my idea to the boys and together we write the verse.

On the way, this guy called Matthew Vaughn calls. He's written his first film after producing a few of Guy Ritchie's early films. He wonders if we'd like to come to a screening the next day. I don't know him but we say yes.

The next day, we go to watch the movie in Golden Square in Soho and afterwards he says, 'I need a title track. Can you help?'

When they put music on a film it's often the last thing they think about. They'll spend $150 million on marketing but the director's calling around trying to scrape together a song a week before it's due out. If he's rung us, you know he's rung five others. Although that's not my cynical response at the time, at this point the idea of one of our songs in a movie is like, 'Jesus!'

I leg it from Golden Square home and by six o'clock I'm playing him 'Rule the World'. 'Do it.'

We fly in John Shanks, who is the insanely talented producer who'd helped us give birth to 'Patience' and our album, *Beautiful World*. The guy who'd judged us first on 'Do What U Like' (remember him?) knew exactly what we were all about by now. He'll go on to produce our next album too, *The Circus*.

We book a studio at Abbey Road and I even get to play its famous Hammond organ on 'Rule the World'.

'Rule the World' is a euphoric song, which uses the old minor verse, major chorus trick. It's actually in D, though I would have played it in C and transposed it up.

'Rule the World' had a no-messing, easy birth – it was barely a week between David coming to the dressing room in Madrid and us pressing 'send' on the track from the Abbey Road studio.

It never got to number one, but it spent nearly two years in the charts. We play it last, or second to last, on a set list. For a stadium audience, it just works. The first time we played it live was on the *Beautiful World* tour and it went down a storm with the enthusiasm and familiarity usually reserved for old material. It's the ultimate Take That song.

In a way A Different Stage is all about Dad. **I miss him.**

# DAD AND 'BLAZE AWAY'

*Don't play Neil Diamond, play this.*
*(Colin Barlow. Born 1941, died 15 October 2009.)*

Dad only discovered 'Blaze Away' because I played it on the organ. I'd been with Mum to Rushworths to buy sheet music for Connah's Quay because the Welsh always came up and asked me, 'Got any marching stuff, lad?'

They loved a marching number, these 60-year-old Welsh fellas with their pints of bitter.

Turns out Dad loved a marching tune too.

He learned this sitting at the back of the clubs waiting for my set to finish, or listening to me through my bedroom walls. Just as Mum liked 'A Million Love Songs', Dad liked listening to me play this old turn-of-the-century marching song.

When I went for my audition at the Halton Royal British Legion, I had a stack of pop songs ready to go, but Dad had a hunch that the old soldiers at the Legion would especially appreciate 'Blaze Away'. Dad was right, and I got a regular gig there, that would take me all the way to the next step, Blackpool, and then beyond, to that other world we saw on television.

You know the idea of cause and effect, of one action leading to another? I look at Dad's sacrifice to buy the organ, his hunch to play 'Blaze Away', and I see in my silent, kind father a God-like figure.

The way Mum and Dad handled my progress was quite amazing. We all know what pushy parents are like, it's awful to see. My parents weren't pushy, but they never said no. They knew something was unfolding and they let it happen where other parents might have shut it all down or overcooked it.

Honestly, it was exciting. It was exciting for all of us. Even Our Ian was enjoying my success. I'd play these clubs and afterwards, sometimes well after midnight, Mum and Dad would bring me home. If the gig went well we'd buy fish and chips and eat them in the car to celebrate.

I had some grim gigs too, and they came to all of those. Still, Mum and Dad sat, quietly, and watched. If I had a gig in Accrington on a Wednesday night, they never said, 'We don't want to go to Accrington to sit in a working men's club for two hours on a Wednesday night.' Which, to be fair, if you've been to Accrington, would have been more than understandable.

'Blaze Away' appears three times in *A Different Stage*. The organ that he sacrificed all his holiday to pay for, and the tune 'Blaze Away' that I play on it, represent Dad. They're Colin Barlow.

When he died suddenly of a heart attack, I drove to Frodsham in silence. There were phone calls of course, the grim carnival of death was just getting going – all that dealing with funeral directors and the other painful paperwork that grieving relatives are expected to handle. What I mean is, I didn't listen to any music. Music didn't make anything better.

It was only as I tried to plan the perfect show graph, a worthy and celebratory way to say goodbye to my dad, Colin Barlow, that it came to me.

Dad and the marching tunes. He loved them.

They brought the coffin in to 'Colonel Bogey' and he left to 'Blaze Away'.

'Blaze Away' was written in 1901 by Abraham Holzmann. The music sounds old-fashioned to us, partly because it has been adopted by military marching bands, but in fact Holzmann was a pop star of his time, he made popular music, people came to see him perform with his band live. His band was more of a dance orchestra, a big-band-style collection of musicians.

I wrote my album, *Music Played by Humans*, with a similar big band in mind, but I'd never write a song in 2/4 time. From the blues, rock 'n' roll and pop music, to techno and grime, it's almost always in 4/4. Common time.

Holzmann wrote 'Blaze Away' in 2/4 because the first half of the twentieth century was defined by wars, and it was written during a time known for 'war fever'. It's basically a marching song that became a smash hit.

The two-step rhythm of 'Blaze Away' is old-fashioned, one two, one two, one two. The genius of George Harrison might have occasionally played around with 2/4, but George Harrisons don't come along very often. Fundamentally, you won't find 2/4 in any pop music.

It's awkward to play, tricky. In three different keys: C, G and then it ends with a lovely reprise in F.

It's a very old-fashioned cadence. It says keep going, one foot in front of the other, everyone. Let's do this. 2/4 time is not just a marching beat, it's the mood of a time. It's the spirit of Dad, strong, steady, one foot in front of the other. Keep going. Don't complain. What a gift my dad gave me.

My dad liked himself, he wasn't in competition with anyone. He was secure. He'd grown up in a huge family, the youngest boy of six kids. My dad didn't walk until he was 7 because he had diphtheria and then he had crutches. He fell behind and would have been one of those kids in the special class at school.

Yet, despite that start, he was content. Born and died in Frodsham, it was only on a night out in Liverpool that he met my mum. My success was the icing on the cake and he did enjoy it. All of it, from the private planes to the free trifle in the box at Wembley. Being Access All Areas never failed to tickle him in the most charming way. There's a famous picture of him during *The Circus* with his back to the stage while we're on, and he's tucking into a bowl of trifle.

That's all right, he more than did his time watching me back in the clubs.

My mum is a Boomer, one of those people that came of age in the sixties and lived through that musically great time. My dad was different. His hobby was farming. He was ten years older than her, born during the war. These people were known as The Silent Generation. Kids that grew up seen and not heard. That certainly describes Dad. Mum was always the one at the front, she did the talking. But when Dad spoke, it meant something.

You know, it's good to talk, this respect for feelings and mental health is positive. But you know what? Sometimes it's good to just stand up straight, shoulders back, one foot in front of the other – 2/4 time – and get on with it.

It might be unfashionable, 'Blaze Away', but I watch the audiences when the brass band version segues into the organ in the stage show and I see the tears. There is a picture I took of Dad the last time I saw him. It was an odd picture to take of someone. It's just him in profile, sat in a chair and looking out to sea. We used it on the front of the order of service. It was like he was almost considering where he was headed next, not sadly, more in a contented way.

RIP, Dad. In a way *A Different Stage* is all about Dad. I miss him.

# 'THE FLOOD'

*I said, 'Rob, I'm sorry.'*
*Robbie said, 'No, I'm sorry.'*
*I said, 'No, but I'm more sorry . . .'*

Rob and I were making up, batting back and forth with the apologies, both of us trying to prove we were more sorry than the other. I've never had this kind of conflict with any of the others. The only reason I ever say sorry to them is if I stand on their toes in the middle of a dance routine. But Rob and I had been two attention-seekers battling for the limelight and it had got nasty at times.

Rob and me would be at Butlin's if we hadn't found Take That, we're like that. We both live to perform, even though he's a funny one, Rob. He has a love–hate thing with performing, whereas for me it's all love. I said to him once, 'Do you like gigging?' He said, 'I want to run out like Freddie Starr and throw maggots at the audience and run off.' Freddie Starr was a nutty old British comedian, who during one of those ITV *An Audience With* . . . shows suddenly started flinging maggots out into the audience of showbiz stars while announcing he'd taken up fishing. Rob loved the idea of doing that, and in that respect we are totally unalike.

With the apologies out of the way, it was time for us to return to the music.

Sometimes it's more than a song. It's a moment. The song is an event, it's the end of the film, it's the season finale. 'The Flood' is five guys in a room together with their arms around each other in 2010, rewinding twenty years to 1990.

It's bigger than just melody and lyrics because it captures an electric moment. Rob and me hadn't sung together on a Take That single since 'Never Forget' came out in 1995.

It's in two keys, there's a key change in the chorus and then a diminished chord – by moving one note in a chord one or two semitones down – that creates a big sense of drama, an emotional feel, it makes you think something's about to happen. Think of 'Michelle' by The Beatles, or 'SOS' by Abba. The artists that use them are often originally classical pianists, like Matt Bellamy from Muse or Randy Newman.

You don't hear diminished chords that often in pop and it's the first one in a Take That song. It carries you along on a wave. 'The Flood' is the song a stadium crowd sings the loudest. You could just sing that opening line and leave the mike and they'd sing it for you.

We've been a stadium band since we came back, Robbie's a stadium artist, and it's a fact that you start writing for your live shows. Us five knew we had to write a song that we could own together that would work. Those songs are called 'no-brainers' and we weren't going home 'til we'd written one. When you have a repertoire of no-brainers, then you've always got to find the songs that can fit in with them on a set list.

The other great asset the no-brainer buys you is space to do what you want, like 'Patience' on *Beautiful World*. When you're writing an album you can play the no-brainer to the record label and they'll bugger off and leave you in peace, secure in the knowledge you've given them a hit.

# PROGRESS AND ROBBIE

*. . . to look down the line and see those four faces.*

Through the period of my life I had been in Take That in the nineties, daily, constantly, I'd find myself looking down the line at my bandmates so many times, it meant nothing. I'd taken it for granted then.

In 2011 I am looking down the line again. There's us five and behind us a hundred-foot mechanical man we've called Tom – another genius idea from Es Devlin.

I've allowed myself a maximum of ten wows in this book, and this moment deserves two. Wow. We're here. WOW!

There we were, the five of us on stage together again for the first time in fifteen years. It had started in 2009 when Rob and I did what I thought was the hard bit, and that was sit down and eat a shedload of humble pie – even though I was probably on a diet at that time, humble pie was allowed. But that, it seemed now, was the easy bit. The eighteen months of recording, touring and promoting *Progress* was harder.

For a long time we lived in a state of 'will it, won't it happen?' Is Rob in, or out? He was in LA, we were in the UK. There were about a hundred agents, managers, labels, lawyers involved, and don't get me started on the stylists, hair, make-up, PAs, all with conflicting ideas about how things were going to work. There'd been a few visits to rehab. It made herding cats look easy. It was so complicated.

Eventually I sat down with my head in my hands and said, 'How can I get out of this?'

There was only one thing to do. The five of us spoke and decided that there were just two things we needed to think about. Us and the audience. If we could be in the same room after all these years and we could make it work, everyone else in our various camps would *have* to follow.

It was incredible being a five again, and to have Rob's singular energy back in the room with us all as men felt like the circle had been closed.

Rob's really into giving presents. It's just who he is. He said, 'What was your childhood BMX like, and if you could change anything about it, what would it be?'

Oh, that was an easy one. The Raleigh Burner but with the yellow plastic wheels.

He'd found this bloke in Stoke who could remake your childhood BMX with all the original parts. Towards the end of the *Progress* tour, these fantasy BMXs arrived for all of us. And of course, this time, my Raleigh Burner had yellow plastic wheels. Being on those bikes for a few moments we were just kids, messing about.

I remember a few years before, just after the four of us got back together, we did a photo shoot for the German magazine, *Stern*. The photographer, Bryan Adams, got out all these props to distract us while he shot away. There were four bikes, pretty ordinary ones, but the minute we four were on them we reverted to my old BMX gang. Everyone was doing their tricks. On bikes, as in life, Howard was the best, he could do loads of tricks, Jason came up a close second, competing with How. Mark was off doing his own thing, like he always does.

Those gifts from Rob took us all back to being kids again, to messing about on bikes, to simpler versions of ourselves. He gave them to us and we all rode round an empty Wembley Stadium before the show.

I was just so pleased to be back on stage with Take That. Yes, it was bloody complicated, but up on stage with them four was the safest place on earth for me.

# JUBILEE '12

*Dad, I bloody hope you're seeing this.*

A lot happened to little Gary Barlow from small-town Frodsham in the thirty-five years between the Silver and Diamond Jubilees. The kid with no worries, loving life, in his double denim, was tucked away inside a ridiculously busy man.

In 2010 I was invited to pitch some ideas for how to celebrate the Queen's sixtieth year on the throne. I turned up and winged it – I was trying to put together the cat herder's nightmare of *Progress*, and volunteering to fix up the Jubilee gig did not appeal much.

There were a heap of other luminaries in the room and I felt pretty sure I wouldn't be the party planner for the Diamond Jubilee.

But when the time came for me to talk, I was seized by the spirit of Jubilee number one back in 1977, and little double-denim Gaz put his hand up. I had never held back in creative discussions for Take That gigs. If we wanted a hundred-foot man, we bloody well had one. If riding in on a giant puppet elephant would complete the magic, then no one could stop us from having one. Little Gary, loving all the happiness, and big Gary, who has seen *O* at the Bellagio ten times, combined forces.

I got the gig, even though I was already in the middle of the busiest year of my entire life and could well do without this too. But I wasn't going to say no to the Queen, plus I was already pretty excited.

My clearest memory of the Diamond Jubilee was standing between the Victoria Memorial Stage and Buckingham Palace about three minutes before the show started. I looked right and left. On the left was this iconic palace and there's the gates that I clutched and peered through age 6, when Mum and Dad had taken Our Ian and me to that remote, exotic place, London.

I'd driven past it a thousand times. I looked over and did one of those impromptu smiles that tugs at your heart, that you feel in your gut. The focus of all these grand state occasions I'd watched on telly, and now I'm here, doing this. It's both mad and magnificent.

And then to the right, my two years of work. A stage that wraps around the Victoria Memorial. It took hundreds of meetings to get permission for that stage, and thousands of phone calls to get all those artists that were going to fill it. The manpower, the frustration, the sheer panic. It was all about to happen. And the world was watching.

In this moment, I'd suspended all the panic and felt complete calm because at this point there was nothing more I could do. All the micromanaging was over.

I realised this and was flooded with a sense of relief. I remember clasping my hands together and saying a little prayer even though I am not at all religious. The only other time I do this is when a plane's about to take off.

Crew, musicians and artists wandered past me but it was all in slow motion, the sound was all muffled, it's like I was observing the whole thing through a camera lens.

The red arrows broke the spell. They roared through the moment.

We all cheered. The event was happening.

The Diamond Jubilee show was the sum of three decades of experience.

I pulled out the show graph, of course.

We'll start big – the Queen's arrival.

Robbie! Up tempo.

Then into the deep heart of the show – the Queen's song and the Commonwealth all coming together.

Now build build build the drama all the way out. Roll out the legends: Elton. Stevie Wonder. Macca.

What a show graph that was.

These Jubilees bring everyone together – they allow us a moment of happiness, joy, and of being proud of where we live and who we are. It's so much bigger than just the event, it's a moment we all have collectively.

Fifteen million people tuned in to watch the concert on TV. Some were probably using it as background while they were burning sausages and drinking beers in the garden. Others were probably properly sat down and watching.

You'd have to have no heart not to have felt moved by the Jubilee and to this day I still think it is the best thing I've ever done.

# GRIEF

*Some scars you die with.*

It's August 2012. Dawn's gone for a last-minute check-up, one week to go. We're so excited . . . Nursery's complete. Moses basket. Clothes all over the floor. All waiting for the main player to arrive. Dawn calls, something's wrong . . . her voice sounding shaky . . . now this is one of those phone calls where you live a lifetime in a second . . .

Poppy Barlow is the third of our three daughters, the third of our four children. Poppy was stillborn on 4 August 2012. Loss and sadness filled our life, and writing this ten years on, all I can say is that the grief of losing a child never goes away.

As we went into writing *A Different Stage*, the first thing Tim made me tackle was the words I would use about losing Poppy. It was difficult at first, it felt inauthentic. How can you explain what follows the death of a child?

Grief just is, it exists, it doesn't have a shape, it exists like an ecosystem around you.

Grief is constantly changing, and feels different from day to day.

I've read a lot about grief, but never a word that captures how it actually feels.

Written down, it's just words, and grief is all feeling.

POPPY BARLOW

*04.08.12*

*I was somewhere else in the first raw fire of grief.*

*Not that anyone would ever have known it.*

## THE LONDON OLYMPICS, 2012

*The whole world watching . . .*

Moments like the Queen's Diamond Jubilee are once in a lifetime, I never thought I'd experience anything like it again, and yet I was set for another just around the corner. Off the back of the best thing I've done came the biggest sporting event of the decade. Two old Take That collaborators were running the closing ceremony and it was a big show. The theme, 'A symphony of British music'.

Kim Gavin was creative director and choreographer. Es Devlin was doing the design. Take That were closing the show. It was going to be one of the biggest moments in our whole career.

But all this ceased to exist the day my daughter died a week before the ceremony. None of it meant anything at all any more.

But there were three other people there to think about, Mark, Jay, How, and they were having the night of their lives.

I was somewhere else in the first raw fire of grief. Not that anyone would ever have known it. That's where those thousands of gigs over the years kick in. I performed on autopilot.

I do remember finding it grimly funny. I was holding my heart, looking up at the stars, and there were these constant directions in my earpiece. They'd set out this routine for us and every few moments, to my shock, as I was singing the song, there'd be an instruction, 'Look left, look right, step forward, step left. OK, over to the left now, over to the right.'

The scale of an Olympic opening and closing ceremony is huge. Take That might have been the closing act, but we were just four people out of 4,100 performers, and we haven't even counted the athletes and the production crew.

We'd been talking about those three minutes for two years but moments like that are never quite as you imagine them to be. And in the end, you arrive, perform, get off the stage, and the next thing you know you're on the M25 going home. I think I was only there twenty minutes.

A room full of sadness
A broken heart
And only me to blame
For every single part

To be loved
but never loved
To have
but never hold

# Fly high and Let Me Go

## 'LET ME GO'

*The gift of Poppy Barlow.*

The song 'Let Me Go' came out in November 2013 and was the first single from *Since I Saw You Last,* my first solo album since the Clive days. I wrote that album over the year after the Olympics, it's a collection of moments, like any album, a collection of feelings.

There's a song called 'Dying Inside' on the album that perhaps better describes how I felt at that time. But that is not 'Let Me Go', the song I wrote to celebrate Poppy.

Sincerity and personal experience had come into my music with 'Patience'. Creativity, ideas, they appear in all sorts of different guises. In many ways it is just about being disciplined and organised. But when big things happen in your life, then music is like water, it flows out of you, over you, through you.

There are two songs that have truly surprised me, I don't even remember writing them. I look down and there are a load of words on the page. 'Let Me Go' is one of those two.

I could not write a song for her that was weighed down by sadness. For the short hour we spent with her after she was born, we felt briefly all the intense love and joy that a parent feels meeting their new child. The room was flooded with light.

'Let Me Go' is not really identifiably a very me song. It came from somewhere deep inside my mind or right out there in the unknown.

It's my bestselling solo single and I think maybe that is because it is a celebration, it somehow offers hope.

This is gonna take a bit of getting used to

# THE INTERNET, III

*Let the fans decide.*

When I first heard about the social networking site Twitter, I thought it sounded like a crap version of texting.

Then I saw how it gave us a direct line to our audience, so I joined in October 2011. I was hardly an early adopter but I realised that the connection with the fans is what we'd wanted for years.

Jason had been missing in action while we wrote our follow-up to *Progress*. Jay was always a reluctant star and then finally he did it; he told us he wanted to leave.

What to do now?

Twitter is where we turned as a band when Jason said he was off. We three honestly didn't know if we should go on.

Could Take That work with only three members?

We put the question to Twitter and waited for the responses over three days. We'd let the fans decide. If they said yes, we went on as three. No? The End.

We sat biting our nails, those three days dragged as slowly as the Eurovision results coming in.

Fairly unanimously, our family of fans said yes.

We would call the next album, simply, *III*.

Lovely.

I want to start by saying how proud I am of what we have achieved together over the years. However, at a band meeting last week I confirmed to Mark, Gary and Howard that I do not wish to commit to recording and promoting a new album. I have spent some of the best years of my life with Take That and I'd like to thank everyone who has been a part of my journey, including my band mates, who I feel are like brothers to me. Most especially my gratitude goes to all of the good and kind, beautiful and ever-loyal fans of the band, without whom none of this could have been possible.

At the end of The Progress Tour I began to question whether it might be the right time for me to not continue on with Take That. At the start of this year and with my full knowledge and blessing the guys began writing new material. There have been no fallings out, only a decision on my part that I no longer wish to do this. I know how much Mark, Gary and Howard enjoy writing and making music, and they know that they have my full support and encouragement to continue on with what is to be another chapter for the band.

**Jason Orange**

This is a sad day for us. Jason leaving is a huge loss both professionally and even more so personally.

We first became aware of Jason's reservations a couple of years ago but had hoped that by giving him the desired time and space he may begin to feel differently. This has not been the case and we now have to accept and fully respect his decision which we know hasn't been an easy one. When we first met Jason back in the day he was one of the most experienced amongst us and always full of energy and belief in what the band could achieve and we'll be forever grateful for his enthusiasm and inspiration over the years.

**Mark, Gary and Howard**

We were paying tribute to the band, and to where we were; it is a celebration of Take That, this unique vehicle we've all taken a ride on.

## 'THESE DAYS'

*These days are your days on the planet.*

We often remember the facts of an event but not the feelings. The feelings when we wrote 'These Days' in March 2014 were complicated.

We leave the stage in 2011 having done this historic tour. Basking in that rosy glow, I do the Jubilee and loads of prime-time telly. Life's as good as it gets in 2012.

Then, with the band, we'd just done our biggest show ever, *Progress*. We'd sold out eight nights at Wembley with Rob. I knew everyone was thinking, 'That's the peak. It'll never get bigger than that.' That feeling of the show graph making a downturn was only made more acute by the fact that Jason kept talking about wanting to go. He'd always had this idea that the band dehumanised him, he struggled with self-belief. I mean, I know that feeling, I know it. Inside that thought process, it's hard to feel comfortable, ever. There's a lot going on.

Two years on, things have changed. Rob's gone, Jay's rarely in the room. Dawn and me are still lost in our own shifting and complicated grief for Poppy.

Jason hasn't left yet, we've yet to ask the Internet if we should go on as three but the ground feels rocky. We come in to this next album feeling, well, not much. It's very easy to make decisions when things are going well. Now there's this demon uncertainty back in a big way. I hated seeing Mark and Howard feeling that way. I'm not brilliant at processing my own feelings, but it hurts when I see people I love in pain.

This band has always been my safe place, they are sacrosanct, a loved world that if all else fails I can go back to, but now it looks like I might lose that. We don't want to end up like The Drifters or Smashing Pumpkins where there's only one member of the original band left.

It was a very strange time.

The feeling was, 'It's all gravy now. The big event has happened.'

I once asked Christine McVie how difficult it was for Fleetwood Mac to do the album after *Rumours*, which was this huge album that has sold in stratospheric quantities, about 45 million to date. It's spent something like ten years in the charts over the last four decades.

Christine told me she and the rest of Fleetwood Mac didn't know how they could make a record to top *Rumours*; even today she listens to that album and finds it beautiful. She said, 'What comes from success is great adversity. Because where do you go from there?' She describes the band 'struggling' as they wrote and recorded their follow up album, which was *Tusk*. And that's kind of where *Progress* had dumped us. Asking ourselves, How do you follow that?

'These Days' was a real band song, which we all wrote together. We went back to that backing track method we'd used on *Progress* with just Mark, Howard and me hunkered down in Mark's studio at his place in Battersea.

We weren't at the stage of booking studios, we were just rummaging around for ideas. We knew we wanted to do an album, us three, but none of us was really mad for it. We were just fishing around, seeing if we had anything, throwing around ideas in that way we had with *Progress*.

That creative chaos in Mark's home studio gave us three a kick up the arse, and we needed it.

The song started out in C originally, like so much of my music does, and then I transposed it. It's this four-chord wonder, F, C, A minor and G. It felt a bit like a ballad at first but we played around with it and started getting that feeling, that feeling when you know you've written a single, when you can visually see it, the dance moves, the whole energy of the thing, how it would be on stage.

As I've said before, it's like these songs 'get born'.

The lyrics were originally a bit complicated, involving a story about a DJ. When we took a break, then came back to the song, we were like, What's all this unnecessary bollocks? We stripped the song back until it was less of a story and more this kind of philosophical epiphany in retrospect.

Years down the line, I look back and it all makes sense. We were paying tribute to the band, and to where we were; it is a celebration of Take That, this unique vehicle we've all taken a ride on. And it was saying, Seize the day, live in the moment, enjoy what you have right now. Those lyrics are as true today as they were in March 2014 when we wrote them.

The band to me, they're not like family, or friends, or colleagues, they're bigger than any of those things. There's an invisible thread that ties us all together. A pretty bizarre shared history that will always be there. It's band blood. As we've all got older our personal lives demand more and more time. How simple life was in the nineties when we all lived somewhere not far from Manchester, England, under the same rainy skies. So nowadays we barely ever see each other unless it's work related. The geography is an issue. Howard lives a two-hour drive from me, Mark an eleven-hour flight away in LA.

Heading deeper into our fifties, all of us, we can't wait to do another tour. We all love this thing. We've done a hard thing by resting the band. By the time we tour, it will be four years – in pop that's an age. But it was time for a break, and then Covid happened too. We'll be chomping at the bit to come back when the time comes.

Once we had 'These Days' in the bag, it was very chilled writing and making that record. Is Jay coming today? Doesn't look like it. Shame, but might as well crack on . . .

I've tried so many times to understand why Jay left but it's impossible to comment on unless you're that person. We're too old to be cajoling people into staying part of a situation they've had enough of. We said goodbye with a few tears and good grace.

A Take That of three got the thumbs up when 'These Days' went straight to number one and we toured the following year. It was going to be OK without Jason.

The band to me, they're not like family, or friends, or colleagues, they're bigger than any of those things.
There's an invisible thread that ties us all together.

# A QUICK WORD ON THE ODYSSEY BY HOMER

*The actual Odyssey. The Greek one.*

*The Odyssey* is an incredible story first told 3,000 years ago that has been adapted again and again. The Coen brothers' film *O Brother, Where Art Thou?*, for example, or *The SpongeBob SquarePants Movie* are based on *The Odyssey*. Tolkein's *The Hobbit*: based on *The Odyssey*.

It's a big show graph this Odysseus has – a soldier, father, husband, and his ten-year journey home from war, and the demons, pitfalls and pratfalls he must face.

Of course, my story is not exactly the same as Odysseus's. I didn't have to fight a one-eyed giant, Cyclops, but I did work with Clive. I didn't have to face off Poseidon, though for a while, I felt like I was drowning in jealousy for my old bandmate Robbie.

Like Odysseus, we have to keep going, we have to face our demons.

He comes back, as I did not, to find his dog pining to death and his wife deluged with suitors. But what Odysseus returned home to is what I do, every time. Love, home, family.

Dawn, Dan, Emily, Poppy, Daisy, Mum, Dad, Our Ian – who's never minded having 'golden bollocks' for a brother. Howard, Mark, Jay, Rob, my brothers in the band, all the incredible music lovers I've worked with, and then there's the audience, an extended family who've supported us all these years.

What **Odysseus** returned home to
is what **I** do, every time...

Love. Home. Family.

# A NOTE ON C MAJOR

*Even when I play other people's songs I start in this key.*

There's a musician's gag, 'C on and F off'. It's something musicians say to their band, 'Right, let's do "I Will Survive" – C on and F off.'

The truth is, all this rock 'n' roll bollocks is a smokescreen. Musicians are nerds, obsessed by letters and notation and a complex language that is somewhere between maths and Ancient Greek, and that's the way we speak music. Then there's what the Greeks called the muse, which sounds incredibly pretentious. But that describes the moments when you write without knowing you're even doing it. In the cardigan years, C was not a place to feel at home and the muse was not there.

Basically, C is a good place to start because the notes are equal distance apart in a row after middle C. It's like the capital city of the piano keyboard. C is everyone's first chord. You add the C bass note with the left hand if you're a pianist – or the left foot to the bottom pedal if you have an A55N organ.

It's the first note you learn as a kid, and so lovely to play in you can get hooked on it. Rumour has it Billy Joel only plays in C.

C major is what 'A Whiter Shade of Pale' is in, it's where I started. It's home, your hands work equal distances from left to right. Do you see? C!

Elton's favourite is B – all the black notes. I hate playing in B. B feels like work.

Stevie Wonder, rumour has it, will detune a piano so it always plays in the key he wants. That's the reason Elton went on before Stevie at the Diamond Jubilee concert. Elton said to me, 'I'm not going on after Stevie – he buggers about with the tuning.'

Of course Stevie wrote *Songs in the Key of Life*, and the key of life, for me, is C major.

# 'A DIFFERENT STAGE'

*This show's not over until we hear our northern boy sing.*

It's going to sound odd, but I never wanted to write a new piece of music for *A Different Stage*. I hate it when people shoehorn new work in. I've been that person in the audience going, 'Never mind the new stuff, give us the hits.'

But the song with the show's name is a sense of where I am now, as a musician – I'm not a pop star any more. I write music for TV, for stage shows and films, I write musicals.

'A Different Stage' is a pianist's song, there's movement, there's range, and the piano supports my singing in quite a complex way. Where 'A Million Love Songs' has four chords, this song has four chords in one line.

This is a 50-year-old man writing now and this song tells my story musically.

In the early days, when I threw the kitchen sink at my songs in an effort just to prove what I could do, it was about showing off. This time, it's natural. It's just me coming back to being me – plus, it's nearly in C.

# A Different Stage

WASN'T THE START AMAZING?
WE CAME OUT ALL GUNS BLAZING,
POWER AND GLORY, FANFARE AND FURY.
ALL COMERS PLEASE,
STAND AND EMBRACE.
LIFE ON A STAGE,
DIDN'T WE SEE IT COMING?
HEAD HITS THE FLOOR, EARS HUMMING,
HALF CLOSING EYES SEE FACES ERUPT IN JOY AND SURPRISE,
LIKING THE RISE,
LOVING THE FALL.

SUDDENLY A VOICE NO ONE KNOWS
STARTS TO ECHO DOWN FROM HIGHER ROWS.
THIS SHOW'S NOT OVER UNTIL WE HEAR OUR NORTHERN BOY SING.
GET ON YOUR FEET,
STAND IN THE RING.

THESE ARE THE ROUNDS YOU WEREN'T GONNA GET.
HOW MANY REMAIN? COULD BE ANYONE'S BET.
ALL WE KNOW IS THIS SHOW
IS AS FAR AS IT GOES,
OUR LATEST PAGE,
SIMILAR FACE,
DIFFERENT STAGE

TIGHTENING LIGHT.

# THE REPRISE

*What's actually happening is I'm doing another costume change into the outfit that I wore for the most important gig of my entire life.*

I'm going to say goodnight and walk off stage now. But we all know I'm coming back on for the finale, the reprise, the encore, the coda, the false tab – you know, the Surprising Extra Bit which isn't really a surprise . . . I'm going to do a megamix, musician's mash-up and everyone's going to go home happy.

Blackpool 1989! You asked, I delivered!

It's a funny moment, the reprise. You go off stage or appear to close the show and then come back on. Everybody knows what's happening but if you don't do it everyone feels a bit short-changed. It's just this funny traditional piece of audience/artist etiquette.

You didn't think we were going to end it there, did you? You've always got to have the reprise of all the great songs, all the cute titles where the star makes a blooper or that secret bonus track on the CD or the message scratched into the vinyl. The artist needs to reappear.

And anyway, this story's not quite over.

It's a funny moment, the reprise. You go off stage or appear to close the show and then come back on.

Everybody knows what's happening but if you don't do it everyone feels a bit short-changed.

# 'NEVER FORGET'

*The most important gig of my entire life . . . is always tonight.*

I still hope that things will go stratospheric again. There's a fantasist inside people who do what I do, they always want another act. In life, they always want a reprise. I've had one. I'd love another.

'Never Forget' is a poignant song, with glimpses of something unique, meaningful and timeless. The song still sounds enormous and I wrote it in 1994 when I was 23. It came after years of writing lyrically quite boyish stuff from the pop music cliché blender.

Then 'Never Forget' came along, a song that seemed to anticipate what lay ahead. The bumps in a road that would grow steeper and steeper. It came out on 24 July 1995, a few days after Robbie left Take That.

I don't remember poetically thinking about the poignancy of the lyrics. Like with 'Let Me Go', I was seized by something outside of my conscious self. The mind is an extraordinary thing.

You think you're in control of your creativity, but sometimes you have no memory of writing something. It wrote itself. They're not all like that, I can tell you. It's about closing off distractions, letting your mind go off and dream. It's a sort of confidence to just let go, the words and the music are in there.

Writing 'Never Forget' was the first time I managed to capture in my lyrics anything meaningful about life. Except it's not just meaningful, it's a bloody crystal ball.

Would I have done anything different if I had known that 'There's a road going down the other side of this hill'?

Probably not, but I wish I'd learned earlier to acknowledge the power other people can have – in your life, in your work, in everything. I can never take full credit for anything. Writing music can be a solitary activity but turning that music into a record has brought me into contact with some extraordinary talents and it has given me those brothers I turn to on stage.

'Never Forget' is a Jim Steinman production. When that guy makes a piece of music he's just incredible. He put the 'Tuba Mirum' from Verdi's *Requiem* at the top of 'Never Forget' and then added a choir of boys' voices. I mean, WOW (that's my last one, I promise). The song has a massive track count, there are 119 layers of sounds to create an irresistible wall of luscious wraparound sound. It's a real art that, making something sound so big and complex. The guy has great taste. He took 'Never Forget' from a New Jack Swing number to this anthem.

And it's an anthem Take That just own. It's just not a very coverable song, it's not 'Sweet Caroline'. It's ours. And there's no other way to finish a gig.

We've come so far
and we've reached so high,
And we've looked each day and night in the eye,
And we're still so young
and we hope for more,
But remember this.

TAKE THAT

Never Forget

We're not invincible,
we're not invincible, no,
We're only people, We're only people.

# NOTES ON A

# WEEK IN RUNCORN

# NOTES ON A WEEK IN RUNCORN

*A Different Stage opens.*

There's times in our lives when events overwhelm us, when bad news, failure, loss and sadness drive you home. The retreat to home is an animal instinct for safety and comfort. It's where we turn back the years and travel the safe roads we walked down as a child.

The familiar little shortcuts only you know, the tree you once climbed, the graffiti that's been there since before time, the friends and family that have known you forever. I've always travelled back to Frodsham at those big milestones in my life. The end of my first career, I went home. Losing Dad, I went home . . .

This time I went home not to retreat and in need of safety and protection, but to celebrate. I went home for the opening night of *A Different Stage*, the one-man show about my life I have created with my old friend Tim Firth.

Is it an age thing? The older you get the more able you are to look back at your roots and appreciate what they gave you. I never thought I'd be back like this and I'm excited. This is where the whole journey started and this show is a tribute to the people and the place that made me. It's a celebration of all that.

Especially, *A Different Stage* is about my dad. This is better than a park bench in the rain for Colin Barlow. I wish my dad had done a show like this, told me his life story. This is all about Dad.

It was 2018 when I first had the faintest inkling that I wanted to tell my life story on stage in my own words. Nearly four years later I am in my mum's spare room just outside Frodsham. Where else would I stay for the opening week of *A Different Stage*?

Our opening week is five nights and one matinee at The Brindley, a 420-seat theatre in Runcorn. I was born in a hospital in this town fifty-one years ago – Dad carefully drove

Mum the twenty minutes from Frodsham up the A56 to Halton General.

This was my home for thirty-three years, and it will always be 'home'.

All the name checks in the show mean so much here. When I first stepped into the limelight as a singer, it was down to the main act, the 'turn', not turning up after a spillage blocked the M56. How those spillages affected us all!

Before I could put it in front of Runcorn, I needed to show it to my wife and to my mum. There was a fear that Mum might think I was airing the dirty laundry. For Dawn, who longs for a private life, I had those worries too.

Dawn watched it alone one day when we were rehearsing in London. 'You sound more northern, like you were when I first met you.'

Just before we came to Runcorn, we did a full technical dress rehearsal in front of friends and family, and friends of friends. Tim came backstage and gave me fifty, maybe more, notes on my performance just before I went on, and said, 'If you remember three, I'll be impressed.'

That performance was weird, brutal, we did it in a rehearsal studio the size of an aircraft hangar. The next project waiting to load in was a massive Hollywood movie, and here we were with our purposely tiny production rattling around. I felt like a pea on a drum.

That show wasn't bad, it went down well but it certainly exposed more weak points, so Tim and I were grateful for that.

More notes from Tim.

What it really told us, though, was it's time. *A Different Stage* needs a proper audience.

The next day I drive up to Frodsham with the dogs. Our first performance opens at 7.45pm on Thursday, 9 February 2022 at The Brindley.

Mum watched our very last rehearsal, the day before first night, with Hannah, Ian's daughter. She said it was 'fine', according to Our Ian, which is praise from my family.

'Lovely,' is what she said to me, 'I'll come every night while you're here.' She said she found it hard as the time got closer to 2009, knowing what was coming, but she loved every part of it. 'I found it moving but didn't get upset.'

It'll be so good to have her in. Over the last few years I've loved catching a sight of her, grinning ear to ear all the way through our shows. This is the best of it really, the peak Take That madness has passed and we can just enjoy it now.

Thursday comes.

Mum feeds us – me and James Security – a lunch of egg, sausages and sourdough and then Martin, the driver, takes me to the theatre for some final notes with Tim and the production crew.

I arrive and go straight to the stage. At 5.40pm we are doing a quick rehearsal of Blackpool: 'Grab your pint of Greenhall's Mild, and a handful of pork scratchings! . . .' and the strap of the keytar comes off, sending it clattering on to the stage.

'Well, that never happened in Blackpool,' I joke, but here we are, in all seriousness, two hours off an audience and bits are falling off.

Tim's voice comes through the dark, 'Just remember, Gary, everything that happens on stage tonight is meant to happen.'

I joke a bit more. Actually, I feel relaxed.

'You can't be too relaxed, Gary, there are too many corners, too many beats you have to hit.'

It'll be a'reet.

As I am walking down to the stage, I joke, 'There's a fan flying in from Spain, got a four-foot banner she wants to unfurl and she speaks no English.'

Someone says, 'Oh God, no.'

'Calm down, I'm joking.'

It is a tricky one, though. We have no idea how the audience will react. I've done this show for a lot of reasons, not least to scare the living daylights out of myself, but also because I love my audience and I wanted to do something far more intimate for them. The theatres are small, I tell them my life story raw and unvarnished, but I can't interact with them and some will find that frustrating.

My audience and me, we know each other well. Some of them have been in my life for over thirty years. There may well be a bit of shouting and dancing, which isn't really what the theatre is about.

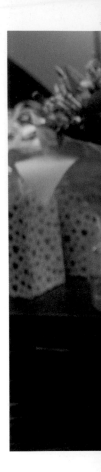

In the theatre, talking is rude, eating is rude, phones are rude, shouting is rude, drinking is rude, I think some people think even enjoying yourself is rude. The culture collision between my audience and a theatre audience is an interesting one. It won't be the first time. When Meatloaf appeared at the Coliseum in 2017 they ran out of beer, for the first time ever probably.

But I'm not going to put rules in the bloody programme.

Some of my audience will never have stepped inside a theatre before. Remember, I had never seen a play until Tim asked me to come and see one of his a few years ago. Sometimes trips to the theatre have you wondering when the interval is, admit it. I saw *The Ten Commandments* on Broadway and found myself counting them off, 'Hellfires, are we only on honouring your mother and father! Another bloody six to go!'

If anyone shouts or 'gets involved', Tim has insisted that I stick to my story. 'If you react, you're going to go way off track.'

It's six o'clock, in an hour they'll open the doors and the audience will start coming in.

Tim is trying to decide at which part of the show to let latecomers in. I want to tell him Take That fans aren't late.

We finish our notes and before I go up to my dressing room I tell everyone I need a moment with 'the room', just me and the theatre. I sit and feel it, the space, imagine the people in there. Then I say 'out' to the few crew in the seats or milling about in the auditorium, 'It needs an audience, I look out here at you lot and it's dead.'

Someone asks if I am nervous.

'Not really.'

'Why are you playing with your fingers like that?'

I look down, 'Like what? Oh, like that.' OK, I am *nicely* nervous.

Up in the dressing room are all my bits for a post-show Negroni. While Margaux helps me with my hair and make-up, Tim gives me a framed, handwritten copy of the words to *A Different Stage*, the song. A first-night gift from my director. I know Tim. As I deliver my words tonight he will be up there, tutting and scribbling notes, wanting it even better.

I'm touched, but we joke around as usual. 'Well, none of this would have happened if you hadn't sent me that video of your guest role in *Heartbeat* in 1999.' (I was famously shit.)

There's flowers. I mention that I once bought my dad a shirt with his initials on it and he thought it was the best thing he'd ever seen.

We're going to have a good time tonight. We bloody better do, I'm missing Liverpool v Leicester for this.

'Remember, Gary,' says Tim, 'it's a story to one person.'

I'm going to make eye contact with everyone in there, every one of the 400 people in. I learned that in the working men's clubs. Always look them in the eye. When someone looks you in the eye it makes them feel special. Seen.

The dressing room's busy. I usually like it that way. When we played the O2 I'd have all the dancers in, bouncing around, but if I did that now I'd be a bag of nerves. It's different, it's meditative.

Don't know why I've got a bloody camera crew in here, I've got to get rid of them. James, Margaux, Clare, a photographer whose daughter is a good friend of Daisy's. My manager, Chris, and Emma from publicity, and someone I've never bloody met before.

Tim's here in the dressing room, telling grim stories. Has anything ever closed on its opening night?

Tim says he knew about a show in NY and when they came down in the interval there was already a 'Closed' poster on the door.

This isn't the O2, I want everyone out of here. On the audio monitor I can hear the audience coming in now. I'd love to know what those people down there in the auditorium think they are going to see tonight.

I need to get into a good head space.

James, James, James, my saviour, he can read my mind. 'Right, everyone out.'

I sit quietly. If I can just get through Act I, I'll be gagging to go out by Act II.

'Right, we need to go down now, mate.'

The stage is on the first floor. I walk down the stairs.

Fuck me, what am I doing here, I must be mad.

It feels like I am going to the gallows.

The riskier it becomes, the more exciting it gets. I am nervous, yes, I am.

The pre-recorded audio of me introducing the show plays and someone pulls the curtain back. 'Ready?' 'Ready, mate.' And I walk on. I blink and it's just me, and them. I start at the piano. My safe place . . .

At the interval it feels like everyone is in the dressing room.

I get dressed for the second half in the cardigan full of balloons that Dawn sewed in for me. Mum's there, she says, sort of sadly but also happily, 'You look so like your dad in that.'

Tim has notes for me, of course he bloody does, including this one: 'Gary, don't bow after a song, it's not the Gary Barlow show.'

Tim and I have agreed on everything, it's been a collaboration, and when he's been brutal on the script, on the direction, on me, I've never doubted he was doing the right thing.

I respect Tim so much, I think he is the cleverest person I know. He's also a very sympathetic and kind man, and he's deeply curious about people, whoever they are. Fame is irrelevant to him. Humanity is what's interesting to Tim.

Fame robs you of your humanity – it can compensate you with some very great rewards ('The money must help,' as my brother loves to say) but you lose something.

Playing Wembley, you can't walk out shy. You've got to boss it. Sometimes I look back at videos and I see the way I stand on stage and I don't like the bravado and the way I stand with my chest out. As I've got older I don't feel like the bravado and the ego suit me. I have chosen to peel off the performance and the puffed-up stadium pose in my life. This show, *A Different Stage*, is all about that. When I dance, one of the things Take That are famous for, it's a kind of dad dance version of those old moves I know so well.

I'm not up there for adoration.

I don't like the fame. I think the fame was what drove Rob to LA, it's why Mark is there now. In Hollywood we are nobody. In London I have a chance to disappear, I can potter round Portobello Road, buying my spices, my ingredients for cooking, but when we set foot outside the M25 people are, I don't know, so pleased to see you. It can stop me going out.

There was this time when Dawn said, 'Babe, we need to go out more.'

The bell rings. It's time for Act II.

I can just imagine what the boys would say if they came to see it. (I've tried to get them down but it's really hard to explain this show without it sounding shit.) I know what they'd say though. One, 'It's only you that'd take this on,' and two, 'Gaz, I think it needs a bit more of you in it.'

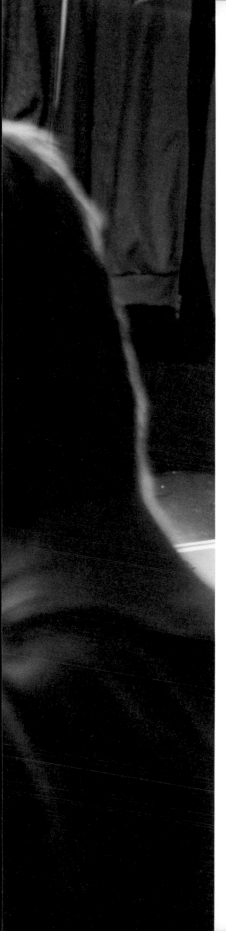

After the show, standing ovations, tears and laughter, I sit at the round mirror in my dressing room, surrounded by light bulbs, taking off my make-up like a proper actor. A proper actor told me to always do this. It's how to shake off the stage and re-enter earth's atmosphere and make sure you don't get a face full of spots.

Yes, that week in Runcorn was magical. Every night a good audience, a great audience. My audience. I love them. They're bloody amazing.

The dressing room is filling up now, I hug everyone. It's emotional.

And then I clear everyone out with the words, 'Right. Out. I want to call my wife.'

I'm writing this, looking back, remembering. Every night was so different. The next night, Friday in Runcorn, the audience was dead noisy and appreciative. Very different to the Sunday matinee audience, who were quiet, but real listeners. I could feel their attention but they weren't noisy. That was a lovely day, it meant I could have my two favourite things, I could do a show *and* go for dinner afterwards. It was weird coming out and it was still light, I've never experienced that before, well, not since the school assembly gigs.

There is just nothing that can replace doing the show in front of an audience, it's the only way to learn and grow. It's why we start the show insisting on no phones or filming. This is a night in the company of someone, me, who's not scared to share everything. Every show that gets ticked off and every audience that leaves the auditorium will breathe new oxygen into its meaning and my connection with it.

I am still getting notes from Tim, tiny little additions, a hand movement, a pause, slight cadence in a word, and as I perform it's starting to feel more and more natural. The parts about my dad and about Poppy, I will never get used to them. They will never be easy. But I power through. No matter if I feel like crying or stopping. It's right, and more brave, to always hold it back. I am telling a story, not asking for sympathy.

Towards the end of the run I feel I am starting to find my authentic voice, Gary the storyteller.

It's harder than you think to be naturally you on stage. It's like my mum when she comes on the phone – even though she's speaking to someone she's known twenty-five years she still puts on this posh voice, 'Hello, Frodsham 33657.'

Tim's tip was to predicate everything I say with the phrase, 'Ey, I'll tell you what . . .' in my head so the words come out more conversational.

Every bit of this journey matters, from the first seed of its creation to every last performance. Doesn't matter if it's a rainy Tuesday or a rowdy Saturday, that's the most important show. That night, that second.

'Standing on the edge of forever' on a nightly basis. It doesn't get much better than this.

# HOW WE MADE

# A DIFFERENT STAGE

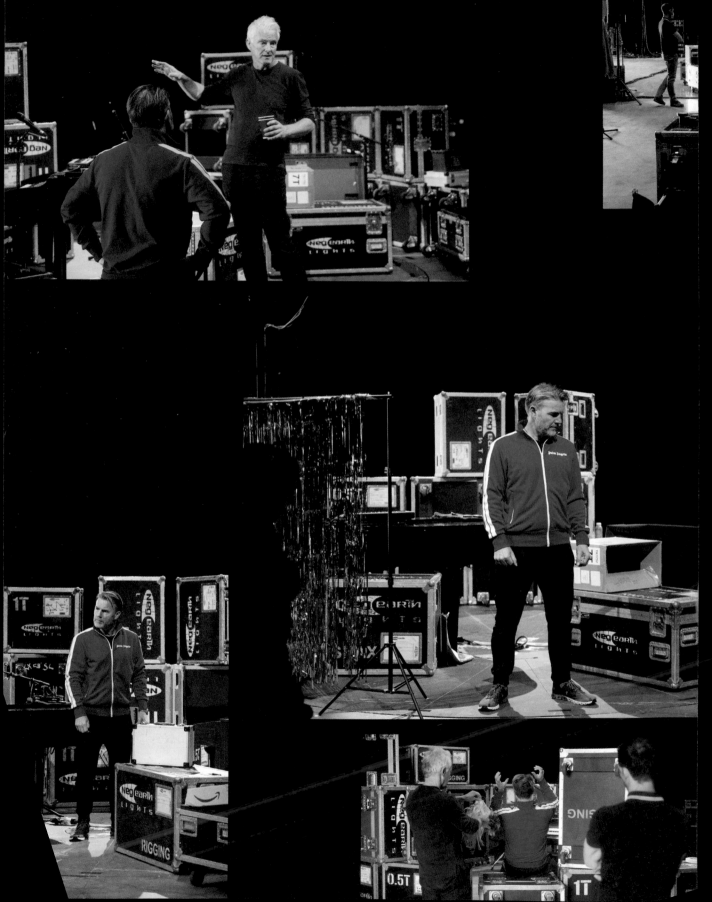

# HOW WE MADE
# A DIFFERENT STAGE

This show is a life story. The words, the emotion, the story, the set, the props, the lights, the sound, the tone in which it's told – deep, deep thought has gone into everything you see and hear. It had to be everything. From the pen to the performance, every element had to be agonised over, I had to give it everything.

I knew, if I was going to do something personal, I couldn't have some producer going, 'Act One is too expensive,' or 'The investors don't like that bit in Act Two.'

I had to sit Dawn down and say, 'Babe, just so you know, I'm going to be spending the kids' futures here.'

I made the decision I would use my own money. *A Different Stage* is my show.

That meant I could work with the people I wanted. My director Tim Firth, the set designer Es Devlin, lighting designer Bruno Poet and sound designer Gareth Tucker are the best at what they do. I love working with clever, talented people.

I've heard people talk about the hierarchy of a production team: producer, director, set designer, lighting, actor, sound, costume . . . blah, blah, blah. I can honestly say that while I am, technically, the actor, writer, producer and the boss, the truth is that at every step of the way *A Different Stage* has been a collaboration.

Working with all these people has been my privilege.

While the production appears relatively simple, there are many tiny details that make the show. Take one small thing, the PS2 portable keyboard, my first, and the one that plays the funny saxophone solo at the end of 'A Million Love Songs'. This simple object had to be completely redesigned, it needed a replacement in case it was faulty – an understudy – and it needed a battery pack that cost three times what the original keyboard cost so there weren't leads and plugs all over the stage. There are so many tiny details that make this show feel like it's just me telling you my life story.

This is the beauty of the theatre.

*A Different Stage* is a one-man show with lots of props, lots of moving parts that I must operate. There are no stagehands; if anything moves, I move it.

What we have is a small and pared-down crew of nimble, easygoing and exceptionally talented people. Take That stadium shows might have 120 people on the production side alone. With this show we are a moving body of ten, one of whom is me. Everything we use fits on one ordinary truck, a Take That show could need fifty.

One of the many reasons I wanted to do *A Different Stage* is as an appreciation for the art and challenges involved in putting together these shows. Now that I understand what's involved, when I go to the theatre I am on my feet before they've sung or spoken a word.

The hours of work, the negotiation, it's incredible. It's expensive, risky, and most people in theatre do not make much money. In the last two years when we were writing and producing *A Different Stage*, Covid was delivering a terrible blow to theatre and it received very little state support.

With this show, I'm paying respect to all that.

Now, I think it's time you heard from some of these incredible people.

# TIM FIRTH
*Co-writer and Director*

Tim Firth is one of the UK's most popular dramatists. He writes for stage and screen, including *Kinky Boots, Our House, Neville's Island* and *The Flint Street Nativity*. He is known for dramatising the extraordinary in British people's ordinary lives.

He was there on the day when Gary's entry to the 1986 BBC 'A Song for Christmas' was 'picked from the sack'. Since a shared train ride back from Pebble Mill studios, they have remained friends and together written two musicals, *The Band* and the adaptation of his box office record-breaking play and film, *Calendar Girls*.

Tim, a father of three, lives near Frodsham with his wife, Kate.

## In one sentence tell me about *A Different Stage*.

This is the most totally unrepeatable project in every shape and form I have ever done.

## What were your goals as a director?

Humility and simplicity were the key words throughout.

## How is it directing someone for a theatre performance who is used to big stadiums and rapturous applause?

If you get the initial intention, which of course Gary does, then it's not hard. We had to eliminate mannerisms more common to a gig, like bowing or acknowledging applause after songs. It finds its own voice as an evening in the theatre and he has to just go with that.

## How do you show the audience that this is not your normal Gary Barlow show?

At the start of the show, it is with the very first interaction he has with the set. Those early moves are critical in letting the audience know the rules.

Four things happen, hopefully imperceptibly, in the first two minutes to set these rules out. First, he walks on doing his own introduction holding a mug of tea. Then he turns his own light on. After that, he changes the words to a known song to tell the audience things are going to be different tonight. Fourthly, he puts the drunk tea 'away' in a box on the set that represents a dishwasher.

By then you should have taken in, rather than being told, that this show is going to be informal, not a gig, that you aren't going to hear the songs as you normally would expect to, and that our set, which is 'just boxes', is going to be our world and behave magically.

### How is it directing a show you have written?

I don't enjoy it. I like being around when a show is being born, I'm there every second sitting in a corner, but I am still watching for flaws or problems in the words. As director, you need to be looking at grand design for its theatrical presentation. I also like plenty of constructive criticism, which directors do not always receive, unlike writers. This was why we did twenty dress rehearsals in Gary's studio for small audiences, to give people the chance to complain about clarity, question our choices and make things difficult in the very best way.

### Were you nervous on the first night?

Yes. Not that it wouldn't work, but that it would lose its shape when a slightly shocked audience, who were expecting something quite different, started to respond to Gary. I can remember fearing the same thing on the first night of *The Band*. We didn't know what the audience would do. I think my memory of that night, hearing the audience respond but then go quiet when they wanted to hear what was coming next, must have given me unwitting comfort.

### Did Gary's performance surprise you? If so, how?

In retrospect, no, because I'd seen it so many times in rehearsal. What impressed me was that it didn't change when put in front of an audience of more than twelve people, all sat quietly. It still feels like that garret performance at his studio.

### What does this show teach us about Gary Barlow?

We spent three years writing a show which pretty much hangs him out there as he is. That is the dirty linen. If you see this show you understand him. You get it. The show is the absolute truth about the colour of his personality. And I say that as someone who's known him since he was 15.

He's not acting. He can't. Watch *Heartbeat* and you'll see that!

### Gary says you love the parts where he is suffering, especially because of Robbie. Why?

It's simply that they're funny lines and he delivers them well.

### What changed when Es, Bruno and Gareth got involved in the production?

It's what didn't change that was most significant. All three understood instantly that the simple show in the garret at Gary's studio was more or less the show as it would be and we had to be very careful about adding anything else to it. They just took the idea and made it sharper, more beautiful, and theirs. All three are true artists, but they are not precious. For example, we tried out a revolving stage for a while. Es said to me, 'Just try it, see if and when it needs it. You never know.' The guy with the revolve sat there at the back for a whole weekend with a big button saying 'go' on it. At the end of the run I said to Es, 'We don't need it.' She said, 'Fine.' The guy took his revolve and went home.

### Explain the importance of set, lights and sound.

The simpler a show is, the more emphasis it puts on each staging and lighting decision. There are areas of the stage which are home, which are the Take That tour van, which are Gary's bathroom in his pop-star mansion and so on, and all we have to create those worlds is, effectively, boxes, sounds and lights. That's the thrilling thing about theatre – you're giving the audience a completed corner of the canvas and their imagination is the brush that does the rest. I love things like the dishwasher drawer, I love the fact that there's a path on the stage that only gets trodden once in the entire evening. When he goes there, for me it's like he's gone up the Khyber Pass. How great is that?

### Gary had been thinking about this project since summer 2018, I think. When did he start talking to you about it and when did you guys start writing?

The first time he floated the idea to me must have been back then. I think we'd been working on it before lockdown, which is when we really got going, so it's been a long time in the making. It benefitted from lockdown in a load of ways. Each section of the story took a couple of months to get into shape, so to have that time was a gift.

# ES DEVLIN
# AND NIKOLAI KUCHIN
*of Es Devlin Studio, Set Design*

Es Devlin is one of the greats of set design. She has lent her genius sculptural designs to all corners of the arts, from Louis Vuitton to New York's Met Opera, and from the National Theatre to the Olympics and the Super Bowl half-time show.

She is the go-to designer for the iconic music artists of today: Beyoncé, Billie Eilish, The Weeknd, U2, Florence and the Machine, Miley Cyrus, Kanye West and, of course, Take That. She designed both *The Circus* and *Progress* tours.

She lives in South London with her husband Jack and two children.

Nikolai was born in beautiful St Petersburg, trained in architecture in Canada and Switzerland and in set design in Berlin. Still young, 29, his work this year alone has spanned contemporary dance in Sweden and highbrow opera at the great Teatro alla Scala in Milan, and Sky's *The Good Doctor* on TV. He is one of four incredibly talented people assisting Es at her studio.

## When did you first meet Gary?

**ED:** The legendary production manager Chris Vaughan introduced us. He'd had an initial scepticism about an opera designer like me belonging in a stadium, but he suggested I meet Take That to discuss their next tour. I met them and heard nothing until a week later when I received an invitation to a follow-up meeting. The invitation came by bike courier and included a flight to Las Vegas. What followed was a very special adventure. Gary had planned every moment of the trip with such care: two shows per evening with a phenomenal meal at a different restaurant every night. All four of the band came along, as well as their charismatic creative director, Kim Gavin. I sensed immediately in Gary a rare combination of humility and talent, and that he thrived on setting the stage for other people to have a great time. We went on to make *The Circus* and *Progress* tours together.

### How was your first viewing of *A Different Stage?*

**ED:** We sat in a small attic room in Gary's studio, a few friends on a few chairs. Gary made a brief introduction then performed the entire monologue. It floored me – and the rest of us sitting there that afternoon: the generosity of spirit, the vulnerability, the humour. I was belly laughing then weeping. It was a special project that I wanted to be part of.

### What were your first thoughts about what the project needed?

**NK:** That it's a very, very personal show and it should feel that way.

### What is the essence of this set?

**ED:** The design itself is almost an antidote to all the designs we had worked on together in the past: no mechanics, no hydraulics – nothing that can go wrong. I think, in a way, it's a medicine for the moments that Gary remembers being stuck up on the giant man's hands or stuck up on an enormous elephant. He said: 'Es, no flames, no revolves, no rain – please – just an honest environment that I can trust and that won't throw me off my purpose of telling this story.'

### How do you create a set that needs to be able to evoke one man's entire life?

**NK:** When a musician goes on tour they will have a pile of flight cases that move with them, and we have used these to make the stage. The flight boxes we have used on stage are, and represent, the relics of the past. These are real flight cases, though they are customised, lots have a grille for speakers, or are soft on top for sitting on. There are twenty-one boxes in total: some are symbolic, some just architecture, and some have to work by turning into something or storing props. There's a box with a slightly raised ramp so that Gary can lean down and easily put on his wig. There is one with a tiny little drawer for storing his whisky in when he's slumped down in the cardigan years. One of the boxes actually contains Gary's inner demons.

It's abstract, you just get the sense that you are looking at an enclosed space where he lives; you can create different spaces, the bedroom, the rocks, on stage, the bathroom.

The centrepiece, though, is the instruments he plays that sit centre stage.

## What is unusual about this show?

**NK:** From a set perspective, it is that Gary operates everything that is on the stage. You will see him switch on lights, operate props, there are so many details, knobs and handles that he activates. Usually there are technicians making things happen. He's his own stagehand. In this respect, *A Different Stage* is almost a magic show.

Another unusual thing is that Gary already knew what props he wanted, and he had sourced a lot of his own props. Usually it's our job and, especially given an artist of his scale, it's unique.

## How would you describe *A Different Stage*?

**NK:** In some ways it's what we call a 'jukebox' musical, in others it's like a play. There's elements of a gig with all this wonderful lighting and sound, and then there are super intimate, very pure theatrical moments. In some ways it's like a magic act. Let's call it a genre-defying theatre piece.

## What might people not understand about Gary as a person or a performer?

**NK:** Gary is so much more personally invested than you might think. I got to work with the artist very closely. We were all exchanging emails, he was very accessible so I really got to know him personally. He replies so quickly.

## How is it to see such a small production?

**ED:** Given the size of those Take That tours, I am as proud of this collaboration as of any of the giant mechanical works: it's rare to witness an artist unpack his life with such honesty and generosity of spirit.

# BRUNO POET
*Lighting Design*

Bruno is a multi-award-winning theatre, opera and music lighting designer with a reputation for versatility. From lighting lakes and entire mountain ranges in the UAE to small intense theatrical pieces like *A Different Stage*, his ability to use light to complement any live performance is unrivalled. He cemented his reputation as a magician with light with *Frankenstein* at the National Theatre.

He lives on the border of Devon and Cornwall with his wife, Annabel, and their daughter, two whippets and two horses.

## What were your first thoughts on *A Different Stage*?

I first saw it in the summer in a small room at Gary's studio. I went with Es Devlin – we collaborate a lot and she invited me along. At that stage there was no technology, just a few props, and it made me really want to recreate that intimacy.

## How did you use light to enhance the intimacy of the show?

We have Gary enclosed on stage by a circle of thirteen 650W Fresnel lenses. The lights frame the stage and fix our attention in towards the centre. They give off a light that is intimate, like a fireside setting, or candlelight, they create a storytelling setting. Humans have a primal connection to the warm sources of light that the show asked for. You want to give the idea that he just rocked up, that it's a show that could pop up anywhere – and in some ways, it actually could.

## What were some of your favourite moments to light?

To echo Gary's great theme of the piece, there's a definite show graph to the lights. There are hundreds of tiny tweaks going on constantly, but I think there are maybe twenty times when we see the lighting really supporting Gary's storytelling.

Take the moment with the pick 'n' mix. We turn all the lights off except one on him and give it a warm sunset quality, so we are really recreating the time and place he ate his sweets as a little boy in the seventies. There he is, looking out at the landscape where he grew up and dreaming of the future 'out there'. We repeat that same lighting much later when he sings 'Rule the World' after the Jubilee and at what is a pinnacle moment in his life in June 2012, looking up at the sky, talking to his dad.

When we're in Blackpool, we make it deliberately kitsch with old eighties disco lights and little cues to help imagine The Talk of the Coast.

The Grammy party is the first time I let the lighting go harsh white. I wanted a totally new kind of light. It's the time we step away from the fireside and step into an alien world. If you talk to Gary about the Clive incident, he will say the light was all wrong, they gave him a bit of a hard white follow spot, a light operated by a human that follows the character around the stage and enhances the 'rabbit in the headlights' feeling. Whenever you make light cooler, you make it less comfortable.

There are so many fun little moments, like when he reveals the Take That T-shirt and there's a brief blast of light to suggest the resurrection of the memory of being a pop star. And obviously we had great fun with the OTT inner demons.

### How was Gary as a 'boss-type' figure?

It's clear he totally gets that theatre works best when it is a collaboration. The most enjoyable and successful shows involve talking, sharing and mutual respect. I work a lot with Andrew Lloyd Webber and Cameron Mackintosh and they are producers with a strong creative presence. I enjoy lighting musicals. My favourite was *Tina*, directed by Phyllida Lloyd: that had a wonderful, easy collaborative energy, even Tina herself was involved – it felt an important show to do.

### How would you describe *A Different Stage*?

Physically a very small production, which tells a gripping story. It has all the qualities a good theatre piece should have. Theatre is about holding a mirror up to ourselves and reflecting what it is to be human. Theatre should leave you feeling different, not bored or worthy.

It's a one-man show and that's tough for any performer. It's really out there, really brave for a Shakespearean actor like Simon Callow to do, so even more brave for Gary because he is such a public figure.

### How did you get into lighting?

First at school. Then I went to Oxford and studied Geography, but in the first week I volunteered for theatre society and never really left the theatre. I went to the National Student Theatre Festival and met Ben Ormerod, who mentored me, and I came to London to shadow him on *A Midsummer Night's Dream*. I went on to work for him, and then for the great Paula Constable, who has won more Olivier Awards for lighting than anyone, ever. While working with them on West End and Broadway shows I was also lighting fringe shows for free.

### In a nutshell, what is the lighting designer's role?

The problem with talking about lighting is it's about trying to articulate something ephemeral. You can't draw it, or model it, it's a leap of faith between director and lighting designer. But, in short, lighting's job is to encourage an audience to look at the stage and hear the story.

### By the way, how do you light a mountain?

This was a project Es and I did in the UAE recently. We lit a reservoir and mountains as part of a celebration telling the story of the birth of nations. I had to light up the mountains after the sun set, which takes 200 lights per mountain. We had a set the size of a stadium, we were shooting lights across a reservoir. No dress rehearsal, just had to go and do it.

# GARETH TUCKER
*Sound Designer*

Gareth Tucker's specialisation is engineering sound for musical theatre, a uniquely challenging field with many moving parts. He has been head of sound on *Hamilton*, *Grease*, *We Will Rock You*, *Spamalot* and Gary and Tim's own *Calendar Girls* and *The Band*.

He found success swiftly when he moved into sound design because as a talented multi-instrumentalist and singer he is able to work with musicians at a very technical and theoretical level that is rare.

He lives in Surrey with his motorbikes.

## Can you remember the first conversations about the sound for this show?

In February 2021 Ryan (Gary's engineer) called and asked if we could do a video chat. I said, 'Yes, when?' 'Now!' I threw a jumper on over my pyjamas and we chatted. I was excited beyond belief when Gary said he was working on a one-man show. It sounded like a very theatrical project.

## You stayed on the tour after first night as sound engineer on the show. What did you learn?

This show is an intricately thought-through hybrid of music and storytelling. I was there night after night as I engineered the tour before the show came to the West End. Tim has a great way of endearing you to the deeper side of a character. When Gary's talking, this is his real life. Still now, after many performances, I'm always hearing new things.

## Who came up with the idea for the devil voice?

I suggested use of the mad devil voice device. Tim, Gary and I would sit and talk about how do we make these moments he battles with inner demons feel different. This was a time for sound to come centre stage. The devil voice is very 'low end'.

When I say something is 'low end', I mean bass. Now with one person, piano and vocals, there's not much low-end sound. An audience really responds to low-end frequency.

## How does the sound change the way we see the story?

This show is an acoustic journey through the way we hear live performance.

It can feel like Gary's chatting to you in one moment, then like he's performing in a concert or a gig, then in a working men's club, or at a party. What I wanted was for all these different sounds to seamlessly blend rather than jumping. So the audience gets this feeling of the journey being very smooth. I used a technology called Space Map Go, which allows me to move from something monophonic, crackly and a bit rubbish to naturalistic to huge and lush like a stadium sound absolutely seamlessly.

Through the sound we can make a distinction between when he is being himself, and when he is telling us the story and more performative moments. An example of this might be when he first sings in public. That segment starts with him slightly hamming it up, 'Here I am playing in the working men's clubs.' It's funny, and the sound is a bit crap, and then suddenly he pulls out the mike, the spotlight moves on to him and he starts to sing. This is a crucial turning point for him in his life. When he starts to sing, the sound instantly changes into high fidelity and what we hear is Gary Barlow! The voice!

## How has this project been different from others?

Usually in the theatre there's not a lot of time because time is money, so you have to accept compromise. This has been different, I've seen it grow and it has been very collaborative, open and free. Every part of the sound is honed – close to perfectly so, in fact.

# PICTURE CREDITS

The author and publisher would like to thank all copyright holders for permission to reproduce their work. Every effort has been made to trace copyright holders and to obtain their permission for the use of copyright material. The publisher apologises for any errors or omissions and would be grateful to be notified of any corrections that should be incorporated in future editions of this book.

37, 47, 54, 55 © Alamy Stock Photo
46 © Haarala Hamilton
80 © Mirrorpix via Getty Images
102, 164–5, 203 © Shutterstock
104–5, 106–7 © Ray Corke
112 © Brian Rasic/Getty Images
113 © Paul Rider/Camera Press London; © Paul Cox/Avalon/TopFoto; © Mike Prior/Avalon
116 © Phillip Ollerenshaw/Avalon.Red
122 © Tim Roney/Getty Images
131 © Dave Hogan/Getty Images
133 © Nils Jorgensen/Shutterstock
134–5 © Pacific Press/Shutterstock
145 © Norman Watson
153 © Jake Chessum
159 © Gary Barlow and © Shutterstock
187 © Cambridge Jones /Contour by Getty Images
188 © Tom Craig /Trunk Archive
191 © Andrew Whitton
197 © Fred and Nick
199, 200–201 © Simon Niblett
207 © Jamie Squire/Getty Images
216–7 © PA Images/Alamy Stock Photo

Additional images © Dan Kennedy, © Claire Kramer Mackinnon, © Shutterstock and © Getty images. All other images courtesy of the author.

Front cover photography by Dan Kennedy
Back cover photography by Claire Kramer Mackinnon
Book design and direction by Studio Fury

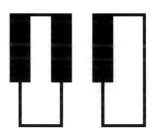